A Dislocated Rib

D. LATRICE

Copyright © 2016 by D. Latrice

A Dislocated Rib
by D. Latrice

Printed in the United States of America.

ISBN 9701408482162

All rights reserved solely by the author. The author guarantees all contents are original and do not infringe upon the legal rights of any other person or work. No part of this book may be reproduced in any form without the permission of the author. The views expressed in this book are not necessarily those of the publisher.

Unless otherwise indicated, Scripture quotations taken from the King James Version (KJV)–*public domain.*

Scripture quotations taken from the Holy Bible, New International Version (NIV). Copyright © 1973, 1978, 1984, 2011 by Biblica, Inc.™. Used by permission. All rights reserved.

www.xulonpress.com

Acknowledgements

There are so many people that kept me going during the writing process of this book. To The Beautiful Ones who always had my back and lifted me up continually in prayer, your love, support, and encouragement is invaluable. To my pastor Bishop Horace E. Smith, a very wise and respected man who leads in our ministry that I am very proud to be a part of. Bishop Smith always reminds us that it is not about us and that is why I live by the motto 'Christ minded and Kingdom focused' at all times. To my co-laborer who spent countless days and nights to make sure that this book was as close to perfection as it could be, it wasn't a walk in the park but we did it, by the Grace of God, we completed *A Dislocated Rib*. To those very close confidants that held me accountable and allowed me to bounce ideas off of them. To my fellow Prophets who gave me what thus said the LORD whether I liked it or not. To all who are a part of me that have been a part of this project to you all I say THANK YOU.

Dedication

I would like to dedicate this book to my children. You have grown to be truly gifted and talented young women who have taken your parents through an amazing journey. I wouldn't change a thing because it was on this journey that life's lessons have shaped us to be the phenomenal women we are today. I want to also dedicate this book to the man who holds my heart. It is you who taught me how to love unconditionally.

Table of Contents

Prophecy xi
Part I: Introduction 13
    The Early Years
    &Separation
    Guilt, Shame, Stubbornness
    This & It
    The Attacks of the Enemy
Part II: Counseling-Knowing Me 41
    Counseling
    Therapy That Counsels
Part III: Uncovered It. 93
    Lonely With a Husband and Left Uncovered
    Protect Your Core
Part IV 123
Part V: Reconciliation. 139
    How I Received a Forgiving Heart

Prophecy

Winter, everyone in my household had a cold. My husband's cold symptoms after some time had passed with the exception of some mild chest pains. He went to the doctor. The doctor asked if he'd fallen, or exercised improperly, or played any contact sports. The doctor asked these questions because after some tests were ran it was discovered that his rib was dislocated and none of the usual things that would cause this type of injury had happened to him. My husband's rib was dislocated and he had not fallen, exercised improperly, or played any contact sports. To fix the problem with the dislocated rib the doctor took his thumbs and pushed the rib back into place.

    I was reminded of a dream that my husband had a few weeks before going to the doctor, my husband had a dream where he was fighting in his sleep. He'd dreamed that he was wrestling with some unknown woman. In the dream he was in a place where he once lived, where the hallway was dark, where some lady [woman] grabbed his wrists, and the unknown woman and he started to tussle with one another [wrestle]. I believe that it was during this dream that his rib was dislocated. In reality, a mistress took my place in his life, dislocating me, his rib. The dream was a prophecy of what was to come in our marriage, and in our lives.

Part I

Introduction

What is this that leads me to this place?
Time comes back with a vengeances taking reality to its breaking point.
I sit on the edge of a deep well that threatens to pull me into a vortex of passion and longing that my heart has never known.
I search for uncertainty and find my answer in the depth of your gaze.
Only a love so pure and explosive is seen in the windows to your soul.
The smile that is given is one of endearing assurances of what is to come.
I look into your eyes to see pools of desire that mirror my own.
As the essence of my entire being surrounds the instrument of life and begins to play a song.

When I first got the idea to write *Dislocated Rib*, it was in the midst of one of the most confusing, trying, discouraging, all around horrible times of my life. I would have never dreamed that I would be in this particular situation. But God has shown me not only how faithful He is, but also who I am. I've learned so many different things about myself through this time of separation that I thought it was paramount to share my testimony with others. In this book I detail all that I learned through the pain of separation. I thought that *Dislocated Rib* would just be about me and my husband, but it is through my experience that I learned that there are different people in different situations that are/were affected by separation. For me it was my children, my finances, my well-being, and my mental health that came into play on that fateful day when the decision was made by me to separate from my husband who'd I'd been with for over 20 years.

The Early Years

My husband and I met in the fall of 1985 in junior high school. It wasn't until high school that I became interested in him. I think that I was more curious than anything else. I thought that he was a cute little chocolate boy and I absolutely loved his bowed legs. For us, our romance if you will, began with us hanging out with the group. I began to see him as more than a boyfriend in the winter of 1988. My great-grandmother passed away and he made sure that I got to her funeral on time. It seems small now, but I can remember how special that made me feel. His actions said to me that he could handle tough situations and that he would be there for me when I needed him. Our first real test of relationship came during our time as juniors in high school. I learned that I was pregnant. My husband was supportive with my decision to have our child. I'd already had a child from a previous experience. My husband assumed the role of father for both my daughters. We did not have sufficient resources, but we decided to stay together and raise our daughters together.

The Early Years

This was when I knew without a doubt that I loved him and did not want to be without him.

I was a tomboy. I didn't like playing traditional girl activities like dress up and dolls. I liked to tree climb, jump from roof to roof of the garages in my neighborhood, and sports. Being a tomboy did not take away my natural curiosity about sex. I didn't see my playmates in a desirable way, but I had a curiosity none the less. In the home of my friends there was a lack of supervision and access to things a thirteen-year-old should not have had access to such as pornography. When my male friends and I went over to our friend's houses with their girlfriends we watched pornography. This sent our young over active imaginations into overdrive. I wanted to know what the fuss over sex was about, except on my first exposure or attempt at sex, I became pregnant. I didn't actually have sex, there wasn't any penetration, and I just rubbed skin against skin and the boy secreted sperm. I was in my second trimester when I found out that I was pregnant. I approached this information in the manner that I approached anything that I didn't understand, I read anything that I could find on pregnancy and parenting. It was never explained to me that sperm can survive and move in a moist environment. I was pregnant and still had my hymen. It wasn't until child birth that my hymen broke. Reading prepared me for what would take place during my labor and delivery but there was nothing to prepare me for the emotional and mental toll that having a child so young would have on me in my future. I viewed it as having a full-time babysitting job permanently. My daughter was born one month after my fourteenth birthday. I knew that God was the only one that could create life and that for some reason he chose me to give birth to my daughter.

Hindsight is 20/20, things always seem more obvious and predictable after they have already happened. In other words, I knew it all along. There's some bias to that, but I believe that there is much truth to things always seeming more obvious and predictable after. As I looked back on my relationship and marriage, my husband and I were not knitted together as a husband and a wife. We had a notion that we had each other throughout our struggles, but in the end I believe that we were comfortable with just *'being'* with each other. In the beginning of our marriage things were pretty rough. I'd heard that the first few years of marriage could be a little difficult, but our difficulties were the first seven years of our marriage. We'd argue about the silliest things. Major arguments would end with my husband leaving for a time or with me asking him to leave for a time. The major issues or struggles in our marriage were that we had limited income, we were raising three small children, and he was leaving home for a time and then returning. These arguments became a pattern that would occur around the same time each of the seven years. We'd often argue about our different activities outside of the home. I spent a great deal of my time at church with our children. I don't believe that it was that he didn't like that we went to church, his complaint was the amount of time that I spent at church. I believed that I was expected to drop everything for him but his plans were almost never changed for me. I often felt like a single parent

The Early Years

because it was always up to me to find a babysitter to watch our children. My husband would not babysit our children, and nothing got under my skin more than hearing him say that he was not going to babysit our children. When I would go away to conventions and retreats I always thought that the reasons he would call were to start arguments with me. I felt at the time that it was the devil trying to distract me by having me to get upset or frustrated with my husband and thereafter I couldn't focus on the Word of God. I thought that the reason why he wanted me home was not so that he could spend time with me, but so that he wouldn't run into me as he did what he wanted to do.

[1]Gary Chapman describes a spouse as "a person with emotions, personality, desires, and frustrations; whom you were deeply attracted to at one point in your lives, whom you had warm feelings [for] and genuine care. So deeply the attraction to each other that you made a public commitment of the others life to one another [as] long as you both shall live." We were nineteen when we got married. I don't believe that there is a certain age where you should or shouldn't marry. But there is a lot to be said to those who get married as young as my husband and I did. We had children prior to marriage, we assumed the roles of an adult, but we were not mature enough to handle the roles of wife and husband in an institution of marriage. The role of a wife wasn't clear to me as there was no father/husband figure in my life/home. The older my husband and I got, the

---

[1] Gary Chapman
Loving Solutions: Overcoming Barriers in Your Marriage 1998

longer we stayed married or just '*being*' with each other, the more we drifted apart. The drifting seemed like a normal progression of our marriage. And although drifting apart seems like a bad thing, for some relationships, sometimes it is the best thing that can happen. I believe that it is only when you separate, remove yourself from situations, things, and people that you can get a better understanding or outlook on the relationship as a whole. In my perspective, a person can be too close to a situation where they don't even see things as they actually are, but as they feel them to be. This is a dangerous place to be especially when you're making decisions. I'd always heard that a person should not make decisions out of feelings and emotions, but to make intelligent and realistic decisions. But it is realistic and intelligent decisions that one believes themselves to have made. This is why I believe that it was only when I looked back on the decisions that I made for or in our marriage that I was able to draw away that my decisions were out of my emotions. I did not make informed/intelligent decisions, I made emotional decisions that I believed were right for me, and I responded emotionally to situations and events in our marriage that proved to be catastrophic. These emotional decisions moved us forward and backwards at the same time from the place where we were supposed to be: married.

In the beginning of our marriage I can admit that I was unhappy. There were times that I'd gone out with my friends or to an event and my husband paged or called me every hour of the hour that I was out. I felt that he didn't want me to have fun. I would cut my night short, go home to my husband and a short time later he would leave home.

The Early Years

And I'd stay home because it would be too late to go back out or I would not have a ride. I had friends who would say that he loved me so much that he didn't want to be without me for any length of time. I had friends who would hang up the phone during phone conversations whenever they heard my husband's voice in the background. I was told no by my friends for different occasions and told to go and be with my husband. I was not invited to places because I had a husband at home. But my friends didn't realize that there were times my husband went out once I came home or after I'd hung up the phone. I needed to be around others so that I wouldn't have to be alone with my thoughts that would spiral down into depression.

There were newspaper listings around the house with apartments circled and the 'D' word divorce was thrown into my face to the point that after only four years of marriage, I went down to the courthouse for divorce papers that I could keep on hand. I started preparing for the day that he would leave and not come back. In our marriage there was a lot of miscommunication, doubt, mistrust/broken trust that I had to work/get through. Being a woman of faith, and believing myself to have trusted God in every area of my life, it never occurred to me that God was in it with me. I tried to be careful with my words and thoughts because words and thoughts have power. [2]Proverbs 18:21, "Death and life is in the power of the tongue:" [3]Proverbs 23:7, "For as he thinketh in his heart, so is

---

[2] Proverbs 18:21
King James Bible

[3] Proverbs 23:7
King James Bible

he:" I understood that it wasn't just about me but about my husband, my household, and my marriage. My husband and I did not learn how to communicate with one another in our marriage. We believed our communication styles to be thee communication style and expected the other to just '*respond*' in the same way that the other was miss-communicating. Our miss-communicating poured over into our perceptions, how we saw ourselves in our marriage and thereafter how we did things in our marriage. It is my belief that the difference in how we saw things and how we did things determined our outcome. I saw myself doing great things for God, my family, my children, and my grandchildren. I saw what I believed to be all the different ways that I could better my life. I saw even how I could better someone else's life, how I could help and influence them in their decisions. I took to heart, I believe, [4]Philippians 4:13, "I can do all things through Christ which strengthened me." How I did things however seemed contrary to how I saw things. In relationships oftentimes that's the very problem. What is seen in the relationship versus what is done in the relationship is contrary to the other. I believe that anyone in a relationship would love to see their relationship as a whole, prospering, fully functioning, living, and loving unconditionally relationship. But what is done? Do you love one another no matter what? Do you make sure that the relationship is strong, prospering, or whole? Do you make sure that everything that is done, is first, in accordance to God's plan for your lives? Do

---

[4] Philippians 4:13
King James Bible

The Early Years

you make sure that everything that is done, is done for the betterment of your partner? Of course, anyone would love to say yes because we believe ourselves to be working hard in our relationships to be whole, prosperous, fully functioning, living and loving unconditionally. In reality however, that is not what we do, because what we see and what we do will always be different when there is a miscommunication. I can remember the first time my husband and I went on a vacation. We left our daughters with a friend and drove to Atlanta. This was the first time since we were married that we would have an extended amount of time alone. He and I talked about everything and nothing at the same time. We stayed with a friend from high school and their wife. I wasn't very fond of the South so when I found out that a friend of mine was also in Atlanta for work, I had my husband to drive me to their hotel so that I could stay with her for the night. My husband dropped me off and later that evening he came back to the hotel and we talked for a couple of hours and then he left to go back to the friend's house. I should have gone with him, but I didn't. I didn't see anything wrong at that time with him going back without me. When I look back, I see two friends, not a husband and a wife. When I look back, I think of how disconnected I was from the relationship. I also see that it wasn't just me disconnected, my husband didn't seem to care that I didn't spend much time with him either. I saw myself living happily ever after and growing old with my husband. What I did however was contrary to what I saw. I did not make my marriage, living happily ever after, and growing old with my husband my goal. This goal was not in the forefront of my mind during arguments, disagreements, and conversations/discussions. As I thought about the dynamic of how we see things versus how we do things, I began to ask how I could line what I saw up with what I did and because I'm a stickler for the Word of God, I asked God how I could line what I saw up with what I did and it not be just a quote of scripture because it sounded good or encouraged me. When I think about all that we went through I had to ask myself the hard question, did you really love him? I asked myself this question because when I look back I think I saw my husband as someone that I needed to rescue. I loved him as a friend, but did I love him the way that a wife should love her husband. I never fully trusted him to take care of us. I often felt like I was raising myself, our children and my husband at the same time.

In the beginning, I believed that we were so comfortable with each other; it was as if we had been married for thirty years instead of three years when we started a routine of going out to eat breakfast at least twice a week. He would get the newspaper and I would sometimes bring a book I was reading. If you didn't know any better, you would've thought we were in our 80's instead of our early 20's. My husband would always work. The times that he didn't work, I worked. The few times when we were both working, my husband and me almost never spent time together. We lived such separate lives that the weekends were spent doing things with others instead of with each other. Don't get me wrong, he was a hard worker. Perhaps, the strong black woman thing, but I always felt like at any moment he would leave so I never got use to him doing much. The day that I told my husband to strap up (wear a condom) if he was going to be out there (outside our marriage) living fowl was the moment that I knew for sure that I had closed off my heart to what I saw as a doomed marriage. In my jaded thinking I would say that it was because he was with his 'other' women, but the fact that we were so disconnected and that that was the norm is probably close to the truth. We had unknowingly established a routine of never addressing our issues and living expecting the other shoe to drop at any time. The one exception was the routine that we'd established for our daughters where we would take our daughters out to dinner on Monday evenings. Valentine's Day, my husband made special for our daughters. He started the tradition of giving our daughters a card with money in it and chocolate. He kept the tradition going when our first granddaughter was born.

The Early Years & Separation

The first few months into the separation, physically I was fine, mentally and emotionally however, I'd shut down. The lines of communication or miss-communication were still open between my husband and me. We didn't talk much, but we were cordial to one another when we did talk. It wasn't until we were separated approximately a year that the gravity of what had become my life took a toll on me. I began to lose sleep; I began to do the day to day tasks almost by rote. I would sit in church and stare off into space. I held conversations with people and did not remember the conversation, despite appearing fully engaged in the conversation. It was as if I was subconsciously willing my mind to blank because the reality of my separation and pending divorce was forever at the forefront of my mind. I had a friend tell me sometime later, that they watched me during service times at church and could tell that I wasn't there emotionally. My friend told me that I looked spaced out. I'd retreated into my own little world where I wasn't forced to deal with the hurt, shame and disappointment that came along with being separated with a pending divorce. April, 2010, my life imploded. I came across some information concerning whom I believed to be a friend. I questioned how to handle the information that I received. I didn't believe myself to be one who wore their heart on their sleeve. I feel deeply for a number of things and I am passionate about a number of things; but letting my emotions dictate things was somewhat foreign to me in this context because I'd spent a number of years suppressing my emotions. I compare what I received to being informed that someone close to me had died. Something that I loved was dying. My marriage was dying. My husband and I had been married for 17 years by this time, together for over 20 years. We'd had a series of separations by this point, but somehow this felt very different. I don't know if it was because I was different.

 I am not one to man bash. I believe that it is disrespectful to oneself when a relationship ends to place all of the blame on the other person. But this time felt very different for me, there was such a finality to it. The death of my marriage. I couldn't wrap my mind around the death of my marriage. Many things went through my mind, I allowed every negative thought in, and I didn't want to hear any comforting words. I didn't want to hear anyone say that 'it's going to be okay' because in reality the people that I reached out to had never been where I was emotionally, I'd never been where I was emotionally. This was a new place for me. I'd spent more than half of my life with my husband. I knew that this time was different. What do I do now? Where is my life going now?

In our home my husband and I lived as roommates. The elephant in the room wasn't just in the room, it'd taken up residence in every area of our home and life. *You are getting ready to separate; you are getting ready to divorce.* These were the thoughts that were going through my head every waking moment. I would love to say that I had my crying moments and then I was done, that I'd picked myself up and was able to move on. I would love to be able to say that and kudos to those who think that that's what they did. But it was a beast for me. It was ugly, nasty, and vicious. It's all those things and more when you face '*it*' and have to deal with '*it*'. There is nothing nice about separation. There is nothing nice about being dislocated. Dislocation through separation is painful. You cannot function as you should. Our conversations were strained. In my mind, I believed that I was thinking that this separation would be like all the other separations. I tried to get back to that familiar feeling because '*it*' happened before. This time, I just couldn't get that since of familiarity that I was used too. I tried desperately to do it because if I could, that meant that this too would pass and we would reconcile and we would be ok, that is until the next time. This was the cycle that our marriage was in and how I saw it was how to break that cycle so that we would never separate again. I'd said the same thing years' prior during another separation. I remembered saying to God during our seventh year of marriage, God ok, this is seven years. This is your number of completion Lord. I won't do this again, we won't have to go through '*this*' again, and we will never have to live like '*this*' again. This is not your will for us to be separated like '*this*'.

I remember saying that with faith and confidence. Ten years would pass before separation would threaten our marriage again. But this separation wasn't familiar, there was a finality to it. But I didn't do anything to change, I tried to be the same as I had been before things just imploded. When I look back I can see that I really just gave up on my marriage. Maybe if I'd fought for my marriage there would have been a different outcome. He didn't move out right away. We continued to live as roommates for two months. Maybe we should have used that time to go to therapy or at the very least, talk to one another. We were both so angry and I was operating completely in my hurt feelings. I can remember running away from home. I drove around with a friend who after some time dropped me off at another friend's house. Looking back, I see that I should have gone home, I should not have run away. I see the foolishness in trying to run away from the problem. I should've given the person I felt responsible for breaking my heart, my husband, the chance to try and fix my broken heart. Just maybe we could have avoided years of anger, frustration, bitterness and un-forgiveness. I didn't discuss what made me leave. I'd developed a proverbial running away from my problems.

Guilt, shame, stubbornness

I remember the day that he left, it wasn't just him leaving, and this was not me just asking him to leave as we'd done in the past. I had to be strong for my child, my child had to be taken care of, my mid-teen child had to be taken of, it wasn't just about him and I. How do I get my child through this? How do I make '*this*' okay for her and still take care of me? As women, often times we will take care of everyone else except ourselves and when we finally get around to taking care of ourselves we are so far gone that we don't think that we need any more help. I thought that it wasn't a good thing for my daughter to live in a home where there was tension or arguing. My daughter was old enough to know that something was wrong. My husband and I tried to keep as much of it away from her as possible, but my daughter knew that something was wrong.

Our children were most important to my husband and me. He and I tried our best to make sure that our daughters didn't lack or want for anything. My husband and I both grew up in single parent households and we always felt like we were ahead of the game because we were raising our children in a two parent household. We didn't want to do as [5]Gary Chapman stated, where "many people in trouble marriages base their lives upon commonly held myths... [One], [that we were a] product of [our] environment because [we] didn't grow up in a two parent, married household. [Two, and because we were not raised in a two parent, husband/wife household that that would be] the reason why [we wouldn't] know how to be both husband/wife, mother/father in a functional household. [Three], because [we] grew up in dysfunction [that was] the reason why there's dysfunction in [our] marriage. [Four], my father was no good, he left me, so I'm no good and I'll leave my wife. [And six], how [we felt] emotionally [was] predicated by/on the actions of my spouse... these myths cause one to feel helpless, hopeless and will lead to depression." Our daughters were definitely daddy's girls. I can remember during birthdays the birthday girl got to choose the restaurant where the dinner would be. I can also remember when the girls were very young, I'd send them to the store with $1 to get potato chips for $.25. When the girls came in from the store they rushed straight to their dad and gave him a bag of chips. When I asked them where my chips were, they would give me the change. My husband and I laughed. It was wonderful to us that our daughters loved their father and that our girls were happy with their dad being there for them. Christmas time was always made special as well for our daughters because no matter what our resources looked like, my husband made sure that our girls got their entire lists or at

---

[5] Gary Chapman
Loving Solutions: Overcoming Barriers in Your Marriage 1998

least three items from their lists. And then he would take our daughters with him to pick out a gift for me. On Christmas morning, our daughters would wait patiently until we woke up to open their gifts. My husband would put the toys together and put the batteries into the toys. I would cook breakfast. After breakfast, he would go back to bed and I'd clean up and prepare to go to church to feed the homeless.

[6]Gary Chapman in *Loving Solutions: Overcoming Barriers in Your Marriage* wrote that, "when parents' divorce, children lose something that is fundamental to their development: the family structure. Children feel rejected, children get angry. I don't think we were concerned about what our many separations were doing to our daughters. I thought that our daughters would be okay. [7]Gary Chapman in *Loving Solutions: Overcoming Barriers in Your Marriage* also stated that, "children feel rejected, children get angry, [because] we are creatures of memory and relationship [and that] we carry the pain of broken relationships for a lifetime, children feel that their childhood has been lost forever, enter into dysfunctional relationships and marriages trying to not be like their parents, trying to do away with the pain of being a child of divorce marrying their fathers becoming their mothers, [because] the effects of divorce linger for a lifetime. But just maybe *our* children weren't damaged as much because nothing was really different at first. What I mean by this is that my husband's work schedule didn't change. There were plenty

---

[6] Gary Chapman
Loving Solutions: Overcoming Barriers in Your Marriage 1998

[7] Gary Chapman
Loving Solutions: Overcoming Barriers in Your Marriage 1998

of times when our daughters would be asleep when he left for work and when he came home from work. During the previous separations he would call before he came over to spend time with our daughters. He still had keys to the house. He was always there for our girls, a phone call away.

And then something even more interesting happened when he'd gone, I exhaled. It was as if I'd held my breath for so long concerning certain situations and things that I finally felt like it's okay to release that breath. To just blow it out, to just exhale. And a peace came upon me. I believed that this peace was a result of the prayers from the people who loved me and cared about me. Our time together wasn't all bad. I think being teen parents and friends took up the majority of our lives and since neither of us grew up the way that we were raising our daughters in a two parent household, we never really accepted or fully understood to accept the role of husband and wife. What we had was a routine that began long before we'd married. In our senior year of high school, the routine was in practice. I'd awake at 5:30am to get myself and my oldest daughter ready for school. After school, I'd pick my daughter up from pre-school, get her home by 2:30pm and then head off to work by 3:30pm. My husband would have gotten out of school by then and would have been in route to my house to watch our girls from 3:30pm to 8:20pm. I rarely saw him on the weekends. We were so busy taking care of our daughters that even when we finally married, the routine pretty much stayed the same. It seemed that as long as our daughters were good then so were we.

'This' and 'It'

I had a new reality. I was single, technically married, but physically I was single. I was separated. This was a different world for me. I'd been with my husband since I was fifteen years old. I spent over half of my life with him. And now I would have to learn to live without him. I felt that I could do the whole I am woman hear me roar, I'm a strong black woman, and I can get through anything. I'd never been alone. I enjoyed it, I liked it, and I thought about the things that I could do that I could not do while I was with my husband. I wasn't hindered, I was trying to get a hold on living single. The majority of my friends were single and some of my siblings were single. I saw that they were able to come and go as they pleased, their responsibilities were different, and I saw those that were single as free. My youngest child was in her mid-teens, and was in most ways independent. I was physically single, I felt that perhaps this was the right thing, a good thing, and that going through a divorce could be the best thing that happened to me. But I was tricked, this was not a time when divorce was an option. And in all

'This' and 'It'

of my feeling free, there was an emptiness inside of me. There was a void, a missing piece that I ignored and replaced with living as a single person. [8]Gary Chapman in *Loving Solutions: Overcoming Barriers in Your Marriage* stated that, [we choose] divorce as a survival technique, as the solution [where we experience] withdrawal, [where we are often] confused [because our] marriage [felt] more like [a] prison." Gary Chapman also stated in *Loving Solutions: Overcoming Barriers in Your Marriage*, [we look for/at] divorce to improve the quality of [our] life, to relieve all [our] stresses, to begin [our] lives anew… [But] divorce is never this, men and women are still angry at their former spouse, still a central, emotional position… [Because divorce] does not mean that you will recover from the hurt… [Divorce is] a deeply painful experience… [There will be] scars [from] divorce… [Divorce] complicates things… [And] divorce does not end contact with one another, the nature of these contacts keep the wounds of a broken relationship oozing…"

I can remember calling and pressuring my husband and really wanting to get *'this'* over with. Being separated was not what I wanted. In conversations with my husband he'd asked if I was really ready to end *'it'*. I responded, yeah, why not? Why hold on? I spoke out of my mouth the end into existence. And that was the trick. One moment I thought that I did not have that much power and in the next moment I felt like I did. Words have power, I spoke *'the end* 'of my marriage and the enemy ran with those words. Sometime had

---

[8] Gary Chapman
Loving Solutions: Overcoming Barriers in Your Marriage 1998

passed as I began to settle into my life as single that my youngest daughter began to act out. I believe that my husband and I both had our part in the confusion and bewilderment during our separation. I wanted to think that he knew, that he'd planned 'it' all along, but I knew that this was the thinking that the enemy wanted me to think. The enemy wanted me to think that he had been playing with me for twenty years and that my husband had always been an adulterous husband, that he'd been lying to me all of these years. The enemy was feeding us that we'd been lying to one another all these years. And then our first meeting after having separated ended with us in the bed, we believed that if we were still in love with each other, then why were we separated? After our meeting, I was on an emotional roller coaster ride. During my up periods, I believed that I'd forgiven my husband and that I could move on. I began to do and think differently. The move on process had begun for me, I believed that it was okay to still love him and remain apart. Moving on being attached to forgiveness that is.

The attacks of the enemy

Low self-esteem which caused a false sense of security and self-assurance. In response, I buried myself into activities, I buried myself into planning. I buried myself.

As I buried myself I felt I experienced some enlightening points where I learned more about myself. I learned what my likes and dislikes were as a '*single*' woman. I learned to do things as a '*single*' woman that I would not have done as a married woman. I believed that things were going smooth. But I was on an emotional roller coaster. During my down periods, I would wake up crying, my heart hurting to the point that I thought sleep was the only thing that could help. The pain robbed me from the sleep that I sought. I had periods where I spaced out at home. I believed that when I went out in public that I wouldn't be able to mask '*it*,' I thought I didn't know how to mask '*it*' so that when someone asked how I was and I'd respond good, they believed me. So even though I didn't know how to mask '*it*,' I'd masked '*it*'. I believed that I was good and I wasn't. My physical separation brought out a little adventurous side of me as well. I went and got a tattoo. Looking back, I wanted to do something so very different from the things that I'd done as a wife. I was grieving my husband, our marriage, and going through the stages of grief. My husband wasn't against tattoos; it was just that I didn't have a desire until the separation to get one. I reasoned that my getting a tattoo was to cover up the tattoo of my husband's name and the gang sign that was on my leg. The first tattoo choice was too expensive and the second tattoo choice was not big enough to cover the old tattoos. And instead of taking that as a sign and leaving the tattoo parlor I decided to put the abbreviate design on another part of my body. The second physical change was the color of my hair and the decision to stop using relaxers in my hair. The third physical change was weight loss.

During the first year of our separation, there were so many ups and downs with communicating or miss-communicating. In times past when we'd separate we'd still communicate or miss-communicate with one another, we talked. In times past, when we separated no one from the outside knew that we were separated. I believed that in times past we functioned separated as if we were together. In times past, we just didn't live together. This year was different, this was huge, and I thought on one hand, your marriage is really over, and on the other hand, you did it, and you can live without him. I didn't have to see him every day, I didn't have to talk to him every day. A hatred had developed, a bitterness was setting in. I was under stress to the point that I'd blow up with loved ones over things that I would not have blown up over prior. On one particular occasion I had a blow up with my youngest daughter to the point that my daughter left home and went to stay in my older daughter's home.

I'd always considered my husband my friend. I could ask him to do things, I could talk to him. We'd agreed that we would continue to communicate about our children while separated. I'd spoken to him about the blow up between me and our daughter and the conversation felt strange, in a bad way strange. I asked him to install an air conditioner, our conversation was strained. I was angry. Angry like the cartoon images where the characters would turn red angry. I had never experienced that level of anger. I was in a very dark place. I was not okay. I was dislocated. I was buried. I was in a location that I should not have been in as a wife. I was not in place. As a result of being dislocated, I did things, said things, and felt things that were not characteristic of who I was. I needed help. I needed to seek some help. The type of help that I needed, in my culture, African-American culture, we don't readily seek help in. Counseling, therapy, or psychiatric help is a stigma in our community. But for me, if I didn't get help, the bitterness, the resentment, the anger and the hurt would consume me. I do not like to be lied to. I exploded. I knew that I needed help. I felt humiliated, I called and apologized to my husband. But I knew that if I didn't get myself together, I would fall. I would fall and I would fall fast, hard, and I wasn't sure that I would come back from it. The apology was hard, he'd done me wrong, he was the cause of my meltdown I felt, but he confirmed what I'd come to know, that there was something really wrong. I was not myself.

Part II

Counseling-Knowing me

I walk with labored steps to a place of happier times.
The time has come for me to let go, but how can I you are my heart?
I stand among many attachments and reminders that you will live on.
Yet with all of this activity I am alone with the reality of my life going on without you.
For months I have been so angry and now I know why
You just gave up and left me, how am I supposed to accept that this had to die?

Counseling

To hear my husband say that I was not myself solidified just how far gone my anger really was. I needed to find the right therapist. I prayed and asked the Lord to guide me in who I should go to. I'd sought out a few therapists. I wanted a Christian therapist. The therapist that I chose, I had a gut feeling that this was the one. This was a therapist that specialized in Pastoral care. This was right for me. I didn't know that the therapist that I chose was from another culture, older, I felt that it was interesting. And then I found that I could talk about anything, God, my marriage, what I wanted for my life, anything. I started therapy twice a week. In my mind I thought that I must have been really jacked up if my therapist wanted me to come twice a week. It was through therapy that I learned more about myself, relationships, how I saw things, how things should be, or how things should be done. I had to dig all the way back to my childhood and deal with who I was, how I was raised, the things that made me who I am and how I could be angry.

A Dislocated Rib

In the beginning we didn't talk about my marriage right away. We'd touch on the subject, but my therapist drew back to earlier events I'd experienced in my life. I learned that I'd been depressed for twenty years. My definition of depression was an unwillingness to eat, or binge eating, a person who had crying fits, or a person who felt really down. I didn't realize how vast the definition of depression was. I'd been depressed from the passing of my grandmother. I was heartbroken and another trauma had been added with my husband and me separating. When my grandmother died, I read. I filled my time with reading any book that I could find. My reading was a form of depression because I wouldn't get up to eat when I should have, I barely slept, the only thing I would do was go to the bathroom. I had functional depression. I continued my normal activities and no one seemed to notice that I'd had a complete break or that I was in a deep depression. My therapist explained the affects that this level of depression had had on my marriage and other relationships, but more importantly, my conversation style in my marriage. [9]Gary Chapman in *Loving Solutions: Overcoming Barriers in Your Marriage* stated that, "living with a depressed spouse whose only communication is negative and critical can be a constant source of emotional drain and leave one feeling depleted of energy." In addition, I didn't realize that my depression was manifesting in my eating habits. In times past, my depression would manifest and result with me sleeping all day or with me reading a book in a day. Depression

---

[9] Gary Chapman
Loving Solutions: Overcoming Barriers in Your Marriage 1998

hadn't disrupted my eating until the separation. It had gotten so bad that I would have gotten ready for bed and remembered that I hadn't eaten. I would snack and then go a couple of days without eating a full meal.

I stressed a lot during the first two and a half years of our separation trying to make sure that my youngest daughter graduated from high school on time and went off to college. There were many times that I had to put me on the back burner so that I could help my child. My youngest daughter never said when my parents separated, no, whenever she talked about our separation she always started the sentence with *when my dad left me*. During this time, I became angrier at my husband because he and I promised that no matter what that we would always be there for each other, for our daughter. I was angry because he went back on his word. I did not like being lied to. I hate it. It was as if I was constantly being fed lies by my husband. It was disrespectful and I felt as though he was calling me stupid. It was insulting to me. How did he continue to lie even though he knew that I knew the truth? I was very angry with my husband because ultimately I felt disrespected. I would rather have been hurt with the truth than to be hurt with a lie. It wasn't the first time that he'd lied to me, but I just figured that with us already being separated and on our way towards a divorce, what reason would there be to lie? In therapy I found out that I never trusted my husband. My actions towards him spoke louder than the words that I uttered. And I believe that my husband didn't trust me either because his actions didn't match his words. I didn't have a role model to show me what a wife was supposed to be or do. I married because I believed that it was right to marry. I didn't want to live together unmarried and cohabitating or shacking. I wanted to be right and to live right before and in the eyes of the Lord. I was advised by my older peers to marry. I loved my husband, but I knew that if I'd had the opportunity to make the decision again, I would not have married so young. I would have waited. I would have waited until I'd grown up. My mental state was not that of a wife, I went into help mode, savior mode, enable mode, I wanted to be everything for my husband that everybody else wasn't. This was not a way to enter into a marriage.

My husband had difficulties that stemmed from his childhood. I had been a teen mother. We were growing up together in a role that neither of us were prepared or equipped for. I had images of what a good marriage looked like in that of my Pastor and his wife (First Lady), other married couples in my church, but not a direct role model. In therapy I learned that from my childhood because I did not have a role model that dictated how I responded towards my spouse in our marriage. Being in a state of depression for as long as I had been, I could not care what he was doing. My reaction was that I didn't have any control over him in the area of infidelity. I didn't care because I couldn't care. I was depressed. My not caring I believed spoke volumes to my husband. We took on the connotations of a number of myths that [10]Gary Chapman in *Loving Solutions: Overcoming Barriers in Your Marriage* spoke of, such

---

[10] Gary Chapman
Loving Solutions: Overcoming Barriers in Your Marriage 1998

as the victim mentality where "our environment affects who we are, but it does not control our outcomes… our reaction to our environment will be predicated on us, our perception and unwillingness to not become our environment. [For] the environment may influence, but it need not dictate, nor destroy our life." Or that, "when you are in a bad marriage, there are only two options–resign yourself to a life of misery or get out. [Or that] the individual becomes a prisoner of his choice… [These are] bondage[s] that needs to be broken, [or that] some situations are hopeless coupled with the corollary myth, hope for others, but not for oneself, this thinking leads to depression and suicide. [Or that] people cannot change [because] once people become adults their personality traits and behavior patterns are not set in concrete people can and do change."

My husband and I had discussions, we would talk. This was the one great thing about our relationship. We would sit up and talk well into the wee hours of the morning. We would talk about anything, but we never talked about us. During our discussions he'd jokingly say, "if this doesn't work out right, I'm just going to be out there." For him, he couldn't trust. He'd jokingly made comments that whomever he dated would have to understand that we came first, I and our children came first. And as crazy as it sounds, I found comfort in knowing that I and our children came first. We'd have discussions where we'd ask what we were still together for, longevity, comfort, or because we didn't want to go out and date again. As I look back, was he telling me all along his fears, inabilities to commit, that he had to find a reason to stay, that he was trying to live a lie and still have me and our children? What was it that he was really trying to tell me in those joking conversations? And was I in a place to hear and respond in a manner that would keep him from any of the things that transpired throughout our marriage concerning infidelity? Those discussions for me now as an adult, still, were light banter. We were two young naïve people. And although we've grown, there was much stagnation in our separated marriage.

I was in therapy. Everything changed for me. I started to see things differently, I saw my husband differently. I learned that I was amped on all the wrong things that my husband did, what he'd done to me, the infidelity, his behavior, how he was treating me. I was so upset and angry at my husband that I didn't see my part or role in the separation. This was a truth that I just wanted to put in the past, a truth that I just wanted to be dogmatic about because of the infidelity. His perception, a lie, was in my past. I wanted a divorce. But I had to take into consideration how I made my husband feel, his feelings I couldn't dismiss. Through therapy as I learned more about myself and how I respond and relate in and to my relationships, I could not feel that he should have been hurt because of the hurt that he caused me or because of the things that he'd done to me. I had to realize that hurt people hurt people. I received a revelation in therapy of getting free once I stopped trying to control and get my husband to believe my truth. I stopped living in the past, allowing my past to show up in my present and dictate my future. My husband's indiscretions, all the things that he'd done and lied about. I had to put it in the past. I didn't realize how much I was living in the past. I didn't think that I was living in the past, I believed that I was moving forward but the reality was that my past was my present and my past was the reason that I made certain decisions about my future.

I didn't have the typical in law relationship with my mother in law. I'd ran into her on one occasion after leaving a therapy session on the bus. I hadn't seen her in quite some time. After formalities, I told her that I was in therapy. Her response to me was in the form of a question, "My son sent you to therapy?" To which I responded a little bit. We continued to converse in conversation, I showed her pictures and we promised to keep in touch. I learned after speaking with my mother in law that I was not the only one to have gone through therapy. And I saw how necessary it was for me to talk about things and to get them out because it wasn't just about me or just for me. There were life lessons that were learned that were to be shared in order to help someone else in addition to me.

Therapy that councils

With these new found revelations I began to council through conversations, speaking engagements, and a blog on Wordpress.com as I continued to heal. On one occasion, there was a mother with two children whose daughters had begun to have children out of wedlock. The mother began to go to church sporadically. She felt that she couldn't show her face in church. I understood how she felt because I'd been a teenage mother. I could see from the vantage point of both the children and the mother. My daughter had also become a teenage mother. A cycle had been repeated with my child having a child young and unmarried. I realized even further that our testimonies can help others in addition to ourselves. [11]Revelation 12:11, "… they overcame him by the blood of the Lamb, and by the word of their testimony;" It's God who is the creator of life, the giver of life. I was a teenage mother, my daughter repeated the cycle, but God entrusted us to bring these children into time. I

---

[11] Revelation 12:11
King James Bible

encouraged the mother with my testimony because in time, through this process of being dislocated, once I was put back into place, the cycle of children out of wedlock and dislocation within the next generation's marriages would cease.

I don't really believe in divorce, but I found myself in the process of a separation towards divorce. I was what is called Black Separated where I was married legally, but my husband and I lived separate lives. In my blog I asked my readers, *What Do You Do?* It is not just the current church that has questions about marriage or who have a jaded view towards marriage. Paul addressed the church at Corinth concerns about marriage, living single, and the appropriate interactions between men and women in [12]1 Corinthians 7:1-6, 10-17,

Now the matters you wrote about: "It is good for a man not to have sexual relations with a woman." But since sexual immorality is occurring, each man should have sexual relations with his own wife and each woman with her own husband. The wife does not have authority over her own body but yields it to her husband. In the same way, the husband does not have authority over his own body but yields it to his wife. Do not deprive each other except perhaps by mutual consent and for a time, so that you may devote yourselves to prayer. Then come together again so that Satan will not tempt you because of your lack of self-control. I say this as a concession, not as a command. To the married I give this command (not I, but the

---
[12] I Corinthians 7:1-6, 10-17
New International Version

Lord): A wife must not separate from her husband. But if she does, she must remain unmarried or else be reconciled to her husband. And a husband must not divorce his wife. To the rest I say this (I, not the Lord): If any brother has a wife who is not a believer and she is willing to live with him, he must not divorce her. And if a woman has a husband who is not a believer and he is willing to live with her, she must not divorce him. For the unbelieving husband has been sanctified through his wife and the unbelieving wife has been sanctified through her believing husband. Otherwise your children would be unclean, but as it is, they are holy. But if the unbeliever leaves, let it be so. The brother or the sister is not bound in such circumstances; God has called us to live in peace. How do you know, wife, whether you will save your husband? Or, how do you know, husband, whether you will save your wife? Nevertheless, each person should live as a believer in whatever situation the Lord has assigned to them, just as God has called them. This the rule I lay down in all churches.

I read this and saw that my husband was an unbeliever that had left our home and because God has called me to live in peace, I was going to let it be so. I was reading scriptures not in their entirety, but pulling pieces from scriptures that would justify my wanting a divorce. I read [13]Matthew 19:1-11,

And when it came to pass, that when Jesus had finished these sayings, he departed from Galilee, and came into the coasts of Judaea beyond Jordan; and great multitudes followed him; and he healed

---

[13] Matthew 19:1-11
King James Bible

them there. The Pharisees also came unto him, tempting him, and saying unto him, is it lawful for a man to put away his wife for every cause? And he answered and said unto them, have ye not read, that he which made them at the beginning made them male and female, and said for this cause shall a man leave father and mother, and shall cleave to his wife: and they twain shall be one flesh? Wherefore they are no more twain, but one flesh. What therefore God hath joined together, let no man put asunder. They say unto him, why did Moses then command to give a writing of divorcement, and to put her away? He saith unto them, Moses because of the hardness of your hearts suffered you to put away your wives: but from the beginning it was not so. And I say unto you, whosoever shall put away his wife, except it be for fornication, and shall marry another, committeth adultery: and whoso marrieth her which is put away doth commit adultery. His disciples say unto him, if the case of the man so with his wife, it is not good to marry. But he said unto them, all men cannot receive this saying, save they to whom it is given.

I read this and saw that I could get a divorce because my husband had committed adultery. I thought cool then I'm in order. But then I began to read with my spiritual eyes rather than my natural or emotional eyes and paused at Matthew 19:8 and realized that divorce was never the will of God in marriages. The two will become one flesh and what God has joined together no one, not even the spouses could separate or break apart.

A Dislocated Rib

You can present an argument on whether divorce is an option in your situation. [14]Gary Chapman in *Loving Solutions: Overcoming Barriers in Your Marriage* stated that the marriage relationship is unique among human relationships and involves deep emotional ties on the part of the husband and the wife... [That] divorce removes some pressures and creates a host of others... [That] divorce should be the last possible alternative... [That husband and wives are to] reconcile [their] differences, deal with [their marital] issues, [and] solve problems. "So sometimes what we think when we are reacting/emotionally responding to problems in our marriages produces unfavorable outcomes. So you cannot enter into a marriage thinking that you can just get out of the marriage if you don't like being married. You cannot just throw away your marriage, you cannot abandon your marriage and start over with another family. When you marry, you marry [15]"for better, for worse, for richer, for poorer, in sickness and in health, to love and to cherish, till death do you part, according to God's holy ordinance." Because once you set it up in your mind that there is an out then you will never fully commit. If you go into your marriage knowing and accepting "till death do you part" then the topic of divorce will never be a topic of discussion. Going into a marriage knowing that you will spend the rest of your life with the person that you are marrying gives you a completely different perspective on what to expect while married.

---

[14] Gary Chapman
Loving Solutions: Overcoming Barriers in Your Marriage 1998

[15] Basic Protestant Vows

And when you are experiencing challenges within your marriage and wondering if you are just supposed to let your spouse continue to do you and your marriage wrong, the one thing that you are not supposed to do as a believer is to have the world's view towards marriage. The marriage union is a representation of Christ's love for/of His church. The church is the bride of Christ. And how Christ responds to His church should be a representation in how we respond to one another in our own marriages. Marriage is unconditional love and forgiveness. God forgives us each and every time we sin against Him. So what if God decided that He wouldn't forgive you for cheating (when you put other things and people before Him)? When you look at things from this stance, it changes your perspectives in what to expect the outcome to be when you are done wrong or experience marital problems. You can do as [16]Gary Chapman stated in *Loving Solutions: Overcoming Barriers in Your Marriage*, "focus on positive actions... [Be] that one individual [that] can stimulate constructive change in a relationship... take responsibility for your own thoughts, feelings, and actions... [Have] an honest appraisal of your life situation and [be the one that] refuses to shift the blame for unhappiness completely on the other so that your actions don't become a part of the problem. [Accept that] I am responsible for my own attitude [that] trouble is inevitable, but misery is optional [that my] attitude has to do with the way I choose to think about things, the difference is attitude. Attitude has

---

[16] Gary Chapman
Loving Solutions: Overcoming Barriers in Your Marriage 1998

a profound impact upon your physical and emotional well – being, attitude affects actions behavior and words, you become part of the problem rather than a part of the solution. [Accept that] I may not be able to control my environment, but I am responsible for what I do within my environment. Attitude influences behavior, attitude affects actions, and actions influence others. I cannot change others, but I can influence others. You cannot change your spouse, but you can influence them. People are relational creatures, they are influenced by all to whom they relate. You can make request of your spouse [but] you cannot manipulate your spouse." When you look at things from these perspectives then your approaches will change, thereby your outcomes will change.

I advise that those who are engaged and planning their weddings to choose their maid/matron of honor and best man carefully. The reason being, if they don't know God and have a relationship with God, then you will need to rethink their position in your wedding. I am not saying that they shouldn't be a part of your wedding, but they shouldn't be your maid/matron of honor and best man. You need someone who is going to hold you accountable for your actions, pray for your marriage especially during the rough times, and to tell you to forgive your husband/wife and to not leave home and/or to go back home. The person that you choose to be your maid/matron of honor and best man should not be supporting or encouraging you when you are wrong or the wrong itself. You need someone who will tell you what is right in various situations that you will encounter as a married couple. Be prayerful about who you communicate with while you are married. Do not allow others to have an unhealthy opinion about your marriage, keep people who do not mean you well out of your marriage. And prayer is always in order for each and every situation that you will come up against. With and through God all things are possible and there is never anything that either of you can say or do that He won't forgive and bring you through. Trust the Lord with/in your marriage. Hindsight is 20/20, these words are from my personal experience, hard lessons learned. I dealt daily with the struggle in remaining faithful to a faithless marriage. I was separated but I was still married. I continued to honor my vows. I was not in pay back mode, neither did I want to do anyone any harm. I also prayed for the 'other' women that my husband had an affair with.

In my blog to my readers I stated that, *Understanding is overrated*. I was trying to figure out why certain things had happened or taken place in my life and marriage. My mind was trying to make sense of things that did not add up. I was thinking about the good and the bad. Graduating from college and separating from my husband who I'd been with for over 20 years. I felt that I'd done everything that I could do to try to make things work in my marriage. I felt that the demise of my marriage was off of me. I began a discussion on Facebook about the root cause of men leaving or acting a fool on good women. I responded that the root cause for both men and women had nothing to do with the man or the woman. The problem I believed was a lack of respect and self-love. You can only give true sacrificial love when you love yourself first. Your mate knows what type of mate they married. Responding positively is key. I cannot say that my husband was all bad, it's just his actions didn't say he knew what type of mate that he had. I'm a phenomenal woman. You cannot make someone a priority that you look at as an option. People cheat because it's what they want to do. It is not something that the other person did or did not do. If that is who they are as a person, then they are going to act accordingly. Sometimes it takes us a bit longer to realize who the person was all along. And it is the response that hurts. But you must choose you. I realized that my biggest problem for years was that I didn't choose me. I put my feelings on the back burner on slow simmer while I took care of the needs of others and I did not know where to draw the line. And when I started asking why certain things were happening to me and didn't get an answer I became withdrawn and accepted that it had to be something that I did wrong. Through my separation my eyes had been opened to the way things really were. I learned that no matter how hard I tried, I couldn't fight if no one was in the ring to fight with me. I learned that just because someone told me something didn't mean that they would own up to what was said if it didn't benefit them or if it caused them to lose something that they desperately wanted. I learned that it is not all about me in that others can and do suffer from what is said and done by me even if my intentions were good. I began to see that God was turning things around and therefore I didn't need to understand how or why certain things happened. Things were beginning to work for my good. My perspectives were changing. I was separated from my husband, but I was free from emotional blackmail and abuse that the enemy was using during my separation. I had to struggle to make ends meet, but I got to see Jehovah-Jireh provide in my life. My focus was on God and making the necessary changes that He would have me to make in my life first, next myself, third my marriage, and fourth my husband.

In my blog to my readers I stated, *Answered Prayers*. I'd asked my readers if they had ever prayed for something so hard and so much that when they got finished they felt like everything was going to be okay. And then as time went by they saw that they hadn't received an answer to their prayer yet? I replied with a passage of scripture from [17]Daniel 10:12-19,

Then he continued, "Do not be afraid, Daniel. Since the first day that you set your mind to gain understanding and to humble yourself before your God, your words were heard, and I have come in response to them. But the prince of the Persian kingdom resisted me twenty-one days. Then Michael one of the chief princes, came to help me, because I was detained there with the king of Persia. Now I have come to you to explain what will happen to your people in the future, for the vision concerns a time yet to come." While he was saying this to me, I bowed with my face toward the ground and was speechless. Then on who looked like a man touched my lips, and I opened my mouth and began to speak. I said to the one standing before me, "I am overcome with anguish because of the vision, my lord, and I feel weak. How can I, your servant, talk with you, my lord? My strength is gone and I can hardly breathe." Again the one who looked like a

---

[17] Daniel 10:12-19
New International Version

man touched me and gave me strength. "Do not be afraid, you who are highly esteemed," he said. "Peace! Be strong now; be strong." When he spoke to me, I was strengthened and said, "Speak, my lord, since you have given me strength."

The Lord answered Daniel's prayer, but the angel of the Lord was held up and required assistance to get the answer to Daniel. There are going to be times when we will get an immediate answer to our prayers, but then there will also be a battle going on with the one delivering the answer to our prayers. But we cannot give up on what we've prayed for, we have to continue to pray because the one delivering the answer to our prayer may be held up and in need of assistance. We have to cover them in prayer that they receive what they need in order to answer our prayers. I can remember countless times when I'd prayed about something and felt really good about it and I just knew that God answered right then but I just didn't see the manifestation of my answer. I found it very interesting that the angel of the Lord was held up and did not ask for help right away. Could it be that we were to build up our faith during the waiting time. Perhaps God used that waiting time to teach us the lesson that He would release what He had for us when we were able to handle it. Another interesting point was that when the angel did call for help he called for the Archangel Michael. That let me know that there are some times when God will release the big guns sort of speak to make sure that we get an answer to our prayers. The devil does not want to see our prayers answered. Especially when we are praying prayers of reconciliation and healing for our troubled marriages.

The devil will send all kinds of distractions and obstacles to keep us from praying and from believing that our prayers are answered. So the next time you pray and don't receive an answer right away, know that it has been answered and that there just may be a battle going on for its release to you.

In my blog I stated to my readers, *Take Responsibility for your Actions*. I'd been venting about my marriage, separation, and wanting a divorce, but I knew that it took two to make something go right and wrong. I would have been a hypocrite to say that I was innocent of any wrong doings in my marriage. Sin is sin. I felt that infidelity wasn't for me, but how many times had I not been submissive to my husband and to the Lord? I hated to see women disrespect men in public, but I didn't have a problem disrespecting my husband behind closed doors. There were times where I didn't feel like taking on the responsibility of a wife or mother. I married young, too young. I got that men and woman were different but if I could keep myself together and not give my body to anyone other than my husband, then I felt that my husband should have been able to do the same. During my separation I was presented with opportunities to do some things with men I'd known or had just met, and my flesh wanted me to do some things with those men, but I realized I would have been hurting me first and my marriage. I couldn't reason with myself that just because my husband committed adultery I should commit adultery. Yes, I was separated, but that did not make infidelity right.

I texted my husband during one of the opportunities presented to me and blamed him for what could have happened to me because I

A Dislocated Rib

felt that he'd left me uncovered. I knew how vulnerable I was and Satan knew how vulnerable I was even more so. I was learning *'this'* thing as I went along during my separation. I had some really rough days. There were some things that I didn't understand like how you could spend over half of your life with someone, but hate them? Or why did I have to still be attached when it was obvious *'this'* thing was done. I didn't have the answers but I continued to trust God even when I couldn't trace Him. I felt that there had to be something totally awesome coming my way for the warfare to be as thick and ongoing as it was. I wanted to get *'this'* thing right so that the next time I could be the wife that God desired for me to be and the wife that my husband needed. I continued to go through, but I knew that God was in control. I get that now and while I don't like what I see, had seen, or the path that I knew I had to take, I had to take that I loved the Lord more, so that nothing mattered but Him and being who He had called and positioned me to be. I could not have any pride, so I had to lay before the Lord naked and unashamed of who I was, who I'd become. It was a very trying place to be but I couldn't care about what people thought about *'it'* or even what I thought of *'it'* for that matter. I had to learn that true forgiveness was when a person was restored back to a place in one's life before they wronged you; and that forgiveness was a place where you didn't remember the offense anymore. If Jesus could forgive me and throw my sins into the sea of forgetfulness, who was I to withhold forgiveness from my husband? True forgiveness was a process that now lives in my heart and I really wouldn't have it any other way.

In my blog I asked my readers, *Are there any real men out there who can tell me the truth?* I'd been posting about the infidelity of my husband and how I'd asked him for a divorce for almost a year. How my husband called me by my maiden name and told me that it was over between us and had been for a long time. I was confused because I had been the one asking almost begging for him to let me go so that I could move on. As early as three weeks prior to him calling me by my maiden name I'd gotten a phone call from him where we went down memory lane. I was very angry because on several occasions I'd said to him that if she made him happy then by all means he should just be with her and to sign the papers and to let me go. He reminded me of conversations where he'd told me he dug himself in '*this*' hole and now he had to be the one to get out of '*it*' and that he really didn't want to sign those papers. I felt that he was stringing me along. I was sure that that was for the mistress' benefit, but why lie? I wanted a real man to explain to me the foolishness that my husband had been saying and exposing me to. If I had been willing to give him a divorce and he obviously wanted to be with the mistress, then why not just sign the divorce papers? It was a no fault divorce for me, I just wanted to be free. He didn't have anything so there was no need for alimony there weren't any assets to get and our youngest was a teenager who could have been taken care of with child support. So for me there really was no reason for him not to sign, so why? I needed someone to explain '*this*' to me. I was in an emotional place and went as far as to tell the mistress all the lies that were fed to me by my husband. But it was only because

I didn't believe that she had any morals, or any self-worth. I felt that anyone who could get with a married man would believe anything that the man said because she was desperate. I figured why be angry about '*it*' if you're getting a divorce especially when everything that was said was the truth.

Divorce is defined as dissolution of an unhealthy marriage. I wanted a divorce. [18]Gary Chapman states in *Loving Solutions: Overcoming Barriers in Your Marriage* that, couples stay married but separated "trying to avoid having a blended family experience by not divorcing and remarrying... trying to avoid the financial constraints." In the African-American community however sometimes we don't divorce, we just Black Separate. It is a common myth that it is cheaper to keep her, thereby it is cheaper to stay married to a person and live separate lives because a divorce would be costly in terms of alimony and child support. But my husband and I didn't have any assets and our youngest was already a teenager.

And it continued to be a progression of foolishness. In my blog I stated to my readers that, *I was a Good Judge of Character*. I'd recently come across some information that gave me a cause for pause. As I continued to deal with the infidelity in my marriage I was told by one of the women that he was having an affair with that she'd known my husband for years and that she had been in his life for quite some time. I wondered about that because my husband and I had been together for over twenty years, since we were 15 and I'd

---

[18] Gary Chapman
Loving Solutions: Overcoming Barriers in Your Marriage 1998

never seen or heard of that woman. I dismissed what she said and moved on. A year and four months later another mistress told me that she'd known my husband for years as well and that they had been in each other's lives before I'd even came into my husband's life. I wondered how two different women could have had the same story about my husband? It made me wonder if I ever really knew him. My first time seeing these women was on Facebook. I was told by my husband that they were friends and that I probably didn't know them because one was the friend of a friends younger sister and the other was someone who grew up in the area where we'd grown up as children, and that sent him a friend request on Facebook. I was wondering if I'd missed something. I wasn't looking to place blame, I wanted answers because I was the one that was saying to my husband to let go if that was what he wanted to do and yet he refused to sign the divorce papers. On occasions he told me that he wanted to come home and didn't want a divorce. And to the other woman, the mistress, my husband would tell her that he was legally separated and we weren't and that he wanted to have a life and family with her.

Hindsight is 20/20. You never confront the other woman and you never allow the other woman to plant seeds of deception in your heart and spirit. Looking back, there should have been a completely different conversation between my husband and me. I practically gave him permission to cheat when I told him to strap up if he was going to be out there living fowl. I was in a place of depression that I didn't realize and therefore did not get help with until our separation. Facebook is a great experience but it is also a place of entrapment if it is not used properly. My husband used Facebook improperly, because of where he was emotionally, he allowed himself to become entrapped. As a wife, it was my place to pray and continue to be a wife and address matters as the Lord permitted them to be addressed. My husband and I were in a broken place and neither of us knew how to communicate effectively without pushing the other over the edge. I kept wanting a divorce and for him to let me go by signing the divorce papers that I'd had in my possession long before our separation. I kept them just in case. And that was not the right mentality to have as a wife, you do not keep divorce papers at hand just in case. And my husband kept having affairs. In a strange and twisted way we were giving the other what they wanted, but we were hurting ourselves, our marriage, our children, and the two other women. As the wife being cheated on you don't want to even think about the other woman, but I had to forgive my husband back to the place before the wrong even occurred and remember it no more. And I had to do the same for the two other women. We were all lied to, we were all deceived. The devil had a field day in all of our lives. I wasn't necessarily excusing the other women's behavior, but I had to forgive. And I had to address the matters that were occurring in my life and in my marriage from another perspective. From a spiritual perspective. I had to get an understanding on all fronts as to what I was dealing with and how to properly address it so that my husband and I could overcome the foolishness and live victoriously as husband and wife.

In my blog I asked my readers, *What do you have on my 40?* I'd begun to ponder about fasting. I knew the principals of fasting, whereas [19]Grace to You describes fasting from the Old Testament stance as "the voluntary abstinence from food for spiritual purposes... voluntary fasting in the Old Testament expressed a mournful, urgent seeking of God in distressing circumstances... profound spiritual urgency... and not... [A]Routine spiritual ritual... [A] Deep dependence on God in times of uncommon anguish. In Joel 2:12-13,

Even now, declares the LORD, return to me with all your heart, with fasting and weeping and mourning. Rend your heart and not your garments. Return to the LORD your God, for he is gracious and compassionate, slow to anger and abounding in love, and he relents from sending calamity.

Fasting was an outward expression of the inward reality of a shattered heart. It was an urgent response of repentance and great humility. It was the seeking of deliverance from a gracious God in profoundly desperate situations. Old Testament fasting presupposes the spiritual realities of sin, judgment, repentance, helplessness, and dependence on God." I pondered when fasting would have been appropriate for my troubled marriage. Fasting and praying was the most talked about but the least did thing in most churches. But for me, I remembered a time when I fasted almost every other week. The Daniel Fast, the no meat fast, the nothing by mouth fast and so forth. I'd heard people speak of fasting a week straight or longer with

---

[19] Grace to You
The Heart of Christian Fasting Part I: Fasting in the Old Testament

no food or water and no pauses in-between. It amazed me because the people that I'd heard this from weren't fasting to get a prayer through or to get closer to God, no, they were fasting just because. The few years prior I'd only fasted when I felt God instructed me too fast. And when fasts were called I participated, but my heart was not in it. I would watch the clock until 6pm so that I could eat. I didn't spend my fast time in prayer or seeking God. I prayed perfunctory prayers. I was only praying because I was supposed to. I realized that I had to fast for my marriage. I hadn't been doing spiritual warfare properly. I'd allowed myself to be distracted and consumed with foolishness. I'd been disobedient to God and I'd lost some people and things that were important to me because of my disobedience. I would take things to the Lord in prayer, but I didn't do any of the things that He instructed me to do in prayer. This had to change. My heart, my marriage, my world was shattered. I'd repented and was at a place of great humility. I was in a desperate situation, my marriage was under attack and I needed the Lord to deliver us and restore us back to Him and to the place of functioning as a healthy and whole married couple.

I began a forty day fast using the biblical principles outlined in [20]Grace to You blog posts, The Heart of Christian Fasting. Matthew 6: 16-18,

Moreover, when you fast, do not be like the hypocrites, with a sad countenance. For they disfigure their faces that they may appear to

---

[20] Grace to You
The Heart of Christian Fasting Part I: Fasting in the Old Testament

men to be fasting. Assuredly, I say to you, they have their reward. But you, when you fast, anoint your head and wash your face, so that you do not appear to men to be fasting, but to your Father who is in the secret place; and your Father who see in secret will reward you openly.

"Jesus' teaching on fasting in the Sermon on the Mount was primarily designed to warn his disciples against the sin of hypocrisy... It's crucial for you to see this as you seek to understand the role of fasting in the Christian life... True worship glorifies God, not the man or woman who proposes to seek Him." Matthew 6:1,

Be careful not to practice your righteousness in front of others to be seen by them. If you do, you will have no reward from your Father in heaven.

I had to take a selfless stance, not draw attention to myself, and fast sincerely for my marriage to be reconciled, healed, and whole. For the first ten days I only consumed one meal a day, the next ten days I consumed nothing by mouth until 6pm, the following five days I consumed only fruits and vegetables, the next five days I consumed only fruit, and for the final ten days I consumed only water. Before beginning a fast, you should always consult with your medical doctor. What I am sharing is something that I did that worked for my situation. I am by no means suggesting that anyone with a troubled marriage go on a forty day fast to resolve their problems. I am simply stating what I had to do in order for the Lord to restore my marriage. During my fast time I prayed and laid before the Lord. I set aside time to read my Bible and other spiritual readings that I was lead to read. And I listened. It was important for me to listen to what the Lord was saying to me concerning my relationship with Him, my relationship/situation with my husband and my marriage.

In my blog to my readers I stated, *Changing Positions*. Some time had passed. I'd been separated from my husband who I'd been with for over 20 years. After the initial shock had worn off I started to deal with the guilt of the reason why my husband left our home. And yet while I was in the most excruciating emotional pain that I'd been in my entire life, I continued to press onward. I began to make physical changes that reflected the changes that were going on inside of me. I began to become the woman that I knew was always there, but due to the depression and emotional distress, I just didn't care enough to bring or to let 'her' out. I set goals for the year and on May 7, 2011, I met one of my goals by completing my degree program and graduating with my first degree. I was dealing with my separation and pending divorce or so I thought. I still loved my husband and was very much attracted to him. Well we were still married and as his wife I had to honor the Word of God and my position as his wife. In [21]1 Corinthians 7:5 it states,

Do not deprive each other except perhaps by mutual consent and for a time, so that you may devote yourselves to prayer. Then come together again so that satan will not tempt you because of your lack of self-control.

---

[21] 1 Corinthians 7:5
New International Version

Afterwards I began to question him about his relationships with other women. You see he never admitted to me that there was someone else at that point even though I knew that there was. Hindsight is 20/20, looking back I realize now that that was not the appropriate time to question my husband about another woman. I am a wife, I am a woman of Faith, and I was supposed to fulfill my marital and spiritual obligations and seek God for the appropriate time to have a conversation with my husband about what I'd come to know. Sometimes the information that we come to know is not for us to confront our husbands directly with, but to confront in and through prayer so that our husband's remain covered. And so that whatever attack the enemy attempts, my husband would be covered even in temptation and weakness because as his wife, I would have confronted the issue in and through prayer. I didn't allow the Lord to create the opportunity to have a conversation with my husband, I responded from an emotional place. My husband did not acknowledge the other woman or the role that she played in his life. And looking back I had to come to understand that the other woman didn't have the role that I allowed the enemy to emotionally give her. I was then and continue to be my husband's wife, the only woman with a true role in his life aside from his mother.

On one occasion our daughter was introduced to the other woman as his friend. It was wrong for my husband to bring our daughter into that type of situation, and it was even more wrong for me to respond in the manner in which I did. On another occasion I had someone that I knew contact me and told me that they saw my husband at a

A Dislocated Rib

restaurant in Indiana with a woman who was not me. The person went as far as to follow the woman into the bathroom and asked her who she was there with to which she we replied that she was with her man (my husband). When you are in that situation your first reaction I assure you will not be to just pray. I felt that I had to address my husband and I didn't know when the appropriate time was to do so, so I took the first opportunity that was presented to me. On another occasion my daughter came across messages from another woman on my husband's social media page, we didn't realize that the social media page was not my own, but that of my husband's. My response was to tend to my daughter and what she was feeling. My response to my daughter was that her father was a man. Not aware at that time that experiences, even negative ones, shape our outlook in our relationships.

From that point on I felt that I was pretty much done with him and I felt that I knew that I wanted a divorce so that I could move on with my life. My husband and I continued to talk off and on and during the month of May when some very close friends of ours lost their son to gun violence. And during that time my husband asked me for more time. And on a number of occasions thereafter my husband asked me for more time. He refused to sign the divorce papers and another occasion he came by the house and showed me a scripture. The scripture was [22]Proverbs 5:20, I went a little further up and read verses 17-20,

---

[22] Proverbs 5:17-20
The Message Bible

Your spring water is for you and you only, not to be passed around among strangers. Bless your fresh-flowing fountain! Enjoy the wife you married as a young man! Lovely as an angel, beautiful as a rose- don't ever quit taking delight in her body. Never take her love for granted! Why would you trade enduring intimacies for cheap thrills with a whore? For dalliances with a promiscuous stranger?

I didn't know what I was supposed to feel, I was on an emotional rollercoaster with my husband. On the one hand he wouldn't give me a divorce and the other hand he would not leave the other woman. His phone was ringing to the ringtone "Miss Independent" by Neyo when the other woman would call and I knew that that was the other woman. I told him after some point that it was ok for him to answer, but I assumed that because my husband had lied to so many people that he didn't know how to be honest with me or anyone else for that matter. He left on that occasion telling me that he'd gotten himself into that situation and that it was up to him to get himself out of it. Looking back I realize that was not the way to have handled that situation, but when you are in an emotional place, you cannot make rational decisions and again I assure you that your first reaction will not be to pray. But it has to be to pray. It was not okay for the phone to be ringing with another woman on the other end, it was not okay for me to tell him to answer, and my husband was absolutely right that he'd gotten himself into that situation. But it wasn't completely my husband. We were young when we married, too young. And I was in a state of depression and didn't know it and my husband was broken from his childhood and the only thing that we were doing was living out our childhood hurts and fears against the other. Everything that we fought not to become, we became. And I had to pray like I never prayed before for God to work on me first, my husband second, and then our marriage.

Sometime would pass before I found myself knowing that I was ready to end it all again. A part of me felt sorry for the other woman because I believed that she had low self-esteem or no self-worth to be with a married man, (my husband) and possibly even in love with him, (with my husband). I'd had interactions with her by this time and I'd told her at one point that she needed to get the full story but I believed her to be ignorant because I felt that she didn't want the full story that she needed to believe his lies. Everything came to a head for me when he came over to the house to install my air conditioner unit in my bedroom. I told him not to lie to me, but he didn't listen. I was angry and I snapped. I did apologize for snapping on him but the lies I just couldn't handle anymore.

Hindsight is 20/20 and I realized after attending Bible Study one Wednesday night that I needed to change my position. I had always felt that I was right and even though I still felt that way I had to stop my actions in how I responded to the attacks of the enemy that were occurring in my husband and I lives. Since he didn't sign the divorce papers I had to stop asking him to sign the divorce papers. I had to stop badgering him. I had to stop focusing on him and what he wouldn't do or what could have been. I had to stop getting in the way of what God was doing in his and my life. I had to stop second guessing good Godly counsel just because it was not what I wanted to hear. I had to stop. If I didn't stop I do not know where my husband and I would have ended up emotionally or our marriage.

I stated to my readers, *Acceptance and Forgiveness*. I'd been on an emotional rollercoaster to the point that when I would go outside, what was going on in my marriage would concern and bombard me emotionally. I would find myself overwhelmed and consumed with what I was feeling about my husband and the other woman. I was battling the decision of whether to divorce or to stick things out. I felt that I came to accept that things were not as I had desired them to be and to forgive myself as well as my husband and the other woman. I believed that I had forgiven them, but going through emotionally, it made me realize that I hadn't forgiven them. I had to accept that it really wasn't anything that I had done to make my husband do what he did. Even with me having said the things that I said, that was not an excuse for my husband to commit adultery. I also accepted that while I felt that I should have been important to him, I realized I wasn't and that more than likely it didn't just happen but that I was never all that important to him in the first place. This is where I'd allowed myself to go emotionally. I allowed the enemy to take me on an emotional rollercoaster. I believed that if I was important then my husband would not have hurt me and he would have never made an excuse to hurt me. I accepted that his and her selfishness was the root to all the hurt and pain that was caused and not what I was supposed to have done as a wife. I accepted that number one was who I was in my own eyes and not in my husband's eyes. I accepted that he would never own up to what he'd done. And for me that let me further know my value to him. I had to call my trusted circle of friends and express to them how I was feeling. I had to forgive in order to continue onward. I'd finally come to the place where I could say that I'd forgiven my husband and the other woman for hurting and disappointing me. I forgave the lies and deceit. It wasn't me, my husband or the other woman; it was the devil and his direct attack on my marriage and on the institution of marriage as a whole. It had been a very trying time for me, but through it all I came to understand the woman that I'd matured into. Acceptance and forgiveness are two things that go hand in hand because before you can grant true forgiveness you have to accept the other person for who they truly are faults and all.

To my readers I stated, *There is No Going Back*. Friends of ours had lost their 22 year old son to gun violence. I was greatly shaken by the news. I cried with the young boys' dad. His death made me look at death and how permanent it was. Often times we take life and our relationships for granted without taking into consideration that tomorrow is not promised to any one of us. I'd been going through a personal battle with my husband. I realized how meaningless on some levels it was when I looked at the entire picture. I was able to say so what to what he said or to what she said and to my rants on how I would never trust my husband again. It was ok that I was talked about because life is too short to dwell in the past. The past could not be changed, it was already done. I refused to hold a grudge or to be stuck in a cycle of what was done. I received brand new mercies from the Lord every day that I drew breath so who was I not to extend mercies to others? I believed that I should have extended true forgiveness to all even if they didn't ask for forgiveness. God forgave me every time that I messed up. I didn't ever want to lose anyone that I loved with our relationships out-of-order. When a person dies, you do not get a do over if the relationship with that person was out-of-order. You can go to their funeral and the cemetery and talk until you're blue in the face about how sorry you are or how you should've done things differently, but they will not hear you. Death is final and there is no coming back. With this realization, I decided to do some things differently when interacting with my husband. I was going to love with everything I had. When I was treated wrong by someone I didn't hold it against the person. I realized that sometimes people had a tendency towards displaced anger and that not everything was personal against me. I had to decide to give people the benefit of the doubt and was not quick to judge people. I began to forgive quickly and more easily. I spoke always from my heart and from a place of love even through my pain. For in my pain I learned to accept and forgive knowing that God had allowed me to go through whatever situation I may have been in. I'm more likely to pray for a person now and I continue to be there for people in whatever capacity that they need me, including my husband. The young man that died was 22 years old and he would not have the opportunity to see his child grow up. But God is in control. Do not let death be your reason for realizing how meaningless some things are and how meaningful a person really is to your life. Do whatever needs to be done to reconcile your differences. And move always in an onward, healthy, and positive direction. Death is permanent and I didn't want to be crying over my husband's grave with all the what ifs and carrying with me always a weight of grief, nor him crying over my grave. I married my husband young yes, but I married him. I love my husband and what we have was always worth fighting for. I just had to change the strategy and the method in which I fought in order to get the results that the Lord had always destined for us to have. It is my prayer that you do the same.

To my readers I stated, *Beware of Becoming Stagnant.* I'd received my degree. But I'd become stagnant. The stagnation was not in what I was doing, I was doing everything that I knew how to do to make my life better. I went back to school, I went to church regularly, and I took care of my home. Being active was not the issue. I had become stagnant in my thinking. I had a transformation in my physical appearance, I'd colored my hair, lost weight, and I'd had a transformation even in how I saw certain people. But what I thought about things seemed to have stayed the same. You may ask what the problem with that was and I guess nothing if you don't want the one thing that is constant in this world: change. I still looked at situations as someone who hadn't been through the worst struggle of their life. I still didn't appreciate the lessons that I'd learned or the lessons that needed to be learned during the test against and for my marriage. What was so bad was that if I didn't learn the lessons the first time around, then I would have to experience the test again. The test may be a bit easier the second time around because you would assumedly know what is entailed within the test, but more often than not the teacher Jesus would put a couple of different questions on the test. One of the things that I learned through the tests that I've had was more patience and how to really live in the moment. Another thing that I learned was that it was okay how I felt even if others didn't feel the same way about a situation that I did. I almost messed myself up by not changing my thinking towards what I'd learned throughout my marital tests. A friend of mine was struggling with whether or not to tell the man that she loved that she missed him. The reason she was so apprehensive was because she didn't want to experience rejection. What if he didn't respond or even worse, what if he didn't feel the same way? My response to her gave me a light bulb moment. I told her if she was telling him those things to get a response from him then to not send it to him. However, I said to her, if you want to send that to him because that is how you feel and you want him to know it then by all means send it. It should not matter how they feel, in whatever you do, do it from your heart. I no longer hold anything in. If I feel a certain way about something or someone, I let them know. Depression, anger, or disappointment doesn't live within me anymore and the only way that I can make sure that depression, anger, or disappointment does not ever come for a visit is to let people be themselves and to not hold it against them when they are themselves.

To my readers I stated, *Change is Good*. Reflecting on my physical transformation and being impressed and proud of the woman that I was becoming, one Sunday afternoon I decided to go and support a friend at their church. So I and another friend went to my friend's church to hear her preach. While at the church, the quest ministers canceled at the last-minute and the Pastor of the church asked my friend if we could fill in for the ministers that canceled. My friend and I agreed to preach after looking at one another with blank stares. We didn't have time to study. We got our assignments and ten minutes later the service began. While praying and asking God what He wanted me to say I had an additional question in mind where I asked the Lord, God what are you doing? I look at my being asked to preach as an answered prayer. During my separation I was doing everything but sitting still and listening to the voice of the Lord. I was so busy looking at my separation as a negative that I didn't see that I should have been using that time to focus on the Lord and what it was that I needed to do to change my thinking and to change how I responded to things. I had to change how I saw my husband and I had to change how I communicated with him and others. I assumed that this would be a bad or difficult thing, but it hasn't been. I'm not saying that it hadn't been a little painful at times. I had to face my failures and the things that I did wrong to bring me to this place in my life. Pride is a powerful foe at times and I had to beat pride down. The biggest change had been me and how I talked and engaged with my husband and others. I'm honest with my feelings and in turn it stopped me from holding things in that in times pass would have had me stressed and depressed. The freedom that I feel now is an amazing feeling. I'm nowhere near where I think I should be, but I'm not where I was as I went through my separation. God answered and continues to answer my prayers. I became more focused on ministry and getting myself together so that I was prepared to do what the Lord said concerning me and my marriage. Change is necessary and if embraced and done correctly yields the results that the Lord intended for your lives. Do not resist or fight the changes that are going to occur in your marriage and in your lives. Know that the Lord is with you and that after the change you, your spouse, and your marriage will be in a Godly place.

One of the things that I had to realize most of all is that hurt people hurt people. This was true between my husband and I and I'd experienced it with a friend who hurt me. I asked my readers, *Is Having Respect for Yourself Important?* I'd found myself thinking about the other woman. I'd given counsel to women who had dealt with infidelity and 99% of the time when the man was the one who cheated the other woman or women seemed to either have low or no self-esteem or just didn't care. I believed that anybody who cheated with a married person was selfish and out for selfish gain, however, I found myself struggling to understand how someone got to the point where they just didn't care about respecting themselves or another person's marriage. I wondered if they were desperate, I wondered how the other woman could continue to put herself in a position to take the crumbs of someone else's committed relationship and try to make a meal of her own out of it. In most cases he will never leave his wife and I couldn't understand why that was okay with them. And in instances where he did leave his wife to be with the other woman, I wondered then if they were leery as to how long it would be before he did the same thing to them? Realistically, he cheated

A Dislocated Rib

on his wife, the one person he decided to make a real commitment with and despite that the other woman was willing to have a piece of him and now she could think that she could be the next Mrs. in his life? Was it that they thought that sex equaled love? Did it ever come to them or bother them that they were coming against what God ordained? I realized that the man was as much at fault as the woman, but these were some of the questions that were on my mind about the other woman. I believed that if you respected yourself then you wouldn't disrespect others. I had the opportunity to speak to someone who had been in a long term relationship with a married man and gained some insight.

One, not every married situation is presented to the other woman as a married situation. Married men who are Black Separated especially do not present themselves as married men in the beginning, it is only after a period of time that the other woman comes to know about the wife that he is Black Separated from. Contrary to popular belief, married men don't always carry signs that they are married right away. They don't go home to their wives and they do spend real quality time with the other woman. This is not the situation for every other woman, because there are situations where married men are sought out by woman because they are married. In instances like this, the married man is sought out because she does not want a committed relationship. This type of other woman is selfish because the only needs that she is concerned about are that of her own. Men lie to both the wife and the other woman. He will have both women in a state where they will be at odds with one another and that is the way that he will want it because this keeps the two women from ever figuring out what his true motives are. Satan is the author of confusion. It is confusion that drives an adulterous relationship. It isn't love that anyone feels in these type of situations, it is merely a distraction to not have to deal with the real issues at hand. The other woman provides an atmosphere where the man does not have to deal with any issues that concern him with his wife. Think of Samson and Delilah's relationship. Men go for a place to lay their head even if it means that they lay their heads in a dangerous situation. All parties want to feel validated and that they matter to one another. Fleshly emotions become involved and because all parties are operating from a sinful place no one is handling the situation in the manner in which it should be handled. The other woman is not operating as a saved individual, she is operating from a truly emotional sinful place. She may lack self-esteem, she may be selfish, there are too many opportunities to be with other men to be desperate, but everyone wants and needs to feel needed. But most importantly, woman have a tendency to think that they can change or save men. And when they enter into or continue in adulterous relationships they do so with the belief that he will change for them and if he becomes their husband then he and she will be okay. There is this rescue syndrome that does not work because more often than not, he will not leave his wife. They believe the lie of Satan that the man is supposed to be with them because the wife doesn't give him what he needs as she can. And for some women they don't care. Adulterous relationships come with no strings attached and no true commitment because if he has a wife then she can be with whomever she chooses. It is a sick and twisted situation to be in, all driven by sin and emotion, all based on a lie, but it is a situation that is faced far too often in our marriages in today's society. There are some women who don't know that the man that they are with is married, but separated. Men will have their own places and live separate from their wives and the only way that the other woman would know that he is married is if she investigates or he tells her. And there are times when a child becomes involved. But what no one wants to see is that everyone involved is self-motivated. You cannot save him. You can't even save yourself. Only God can save. The wife has more at state than the other woman so the concern would fall greatly upon her needs for an adulterous relationship to quickly come to an end.

Mental illness plays a factor as well. Some women and men are not mentally stable enough to put the needs of others above their own selfish needs. Over exaggerated sexual needs also drive men and women into adulterous relationships. Pornography also is something that drives both men and women into adulterous relationships. It is important to take your time in coming to know your mate before you marry them. It is said that people don't show their true selves until after the wedding, but people do give off signs that should be paid attention to that will give you some insight into the type of person that you are marrying. As a married couple you need to have open and clear communications about your sexual needs so that you are pleasing one another and the other is not so easily tempted. And it is nothing that the woman has done wrong if her husband still cheats after having had clear and open communication about their sexual needs and desires.

Hindsight is 20/20. I was angry at the other woman and accusing her of being things that I didn't know her to speak of her as. I was speaking from a place of hurt as the scorned wife whose husband violated their marital vows. But I remembered the comments that I'd made to my husband after I'd reached a place in our marriage where I felt that at any moment he would leave so I never got use to him doing much. I told my husband to strap up (wear a condom) if he was going to be out there (outside our marriage) living fowl. I knew for sure that I had closed off my heart to what I saw as a doomed marriage. In my jaded thinking I would say that it was because he was with his other women, but the fact that we were so disconnected and that that was the norm is probably close to the truth. We had unknowingly established a routine of never addressing our issues and living expecting the other shoe to drop at any time. The shoe had dropped. I displaced my angry onto the other women and found myself struggling to understand the motives and the behavior of the other woman that was in his life at that time. But the motives and behavior that needed to be examined where that of my husband and I. We were disrespecting our marriage. We were not being obedient to God in regards to our marriage covenant. My husband was desperate for something that I was not in a position to give to him because we were young, my husband was broken, we'd established a pattern of miscommunication, and I was in a state of depression that I did not know that I suffered from. So why was I angry and venting about a committed relationship that I'd felt the other woman was only getting the crumbs from when my husband and I were not committed in our marriage as we should have been? He'd said to me in a twisted manner that he would not leave me for another woman. I didn't see the conversation then for what it was. I had divorce papers at hand only after four years of marriage. I invested time during our separation into getting my husband to sign the divorce papers, when I should have spent that time praying, seeking God and speaking to my husband about reconciling our marriage. And I couldn't beat myself up either. My husband's choices were my husband's choices. He could have said no to me telling him to strap up and took real time to seek help with me for our marriage. But I was depressed and he was broken and we made poor choices for how we emotionally decided to handle our marriage. We separated well into our marriage and we lived our lives in separate directions. It was not until the last separation that either of us had come to understand what we'd done to the other, to our marriage and to our family. But God showed us mercy, favor and covered my husband and me. The outcome could have been much worse for our lives, our children's lives and our marriage. But the Lord shielded and protected all of us. And He covered my husband during the infidelity.

So it was not that the other woman thought that she could have a piece of my husband and replace me, his rib, in his life as his wife. Or even that sex equaled love. Our sexual relationship was not in trouble, we knew how to sex with one another. We failed to communicate with one another about the things that needed to be communicated in our marriage. We didn't know how to be a wife and a husband to one another we just got used to '*being*' with each other more so like roommates rather than as husband and wife. I wondered how the other woman could stay with my husband knowing that he was not going to leave me to be with her and stay with my husband and be okay with him remaining married to me? But then I remembered that I was separated and living as if I were single. And it took me some time to come to an understanding of what it meant to be separated. I can't and do not want to imagine what it would mean to another woman about what our separation meant to them. I understand that it is more so from culture that had been established. I'd seen it with my mother where she separated, but remained married as well as with my husband's parents where they'd separated but remained married. Both families remained married, Black Separated and just lived completely separate lives as if they were not married. And here my husband and I were, products of our environment, without consciousness to what was truly happening, living out what we'd experienced as children. I wondered if it bothered the other woman that they were coming against what God ordained: our marriage. But my husband and I were both coming against what God ordained. My husband didn't respect our marriage so why would someone else respect our marriage?

It is always after that you will come to a full understanding of what was experienced. Some things you will laugh at and others will make you cry because you will have realized what the Lord protected you from. Pray that the Lord will cover your spouse, guard your heart and mind, protect you from you and your emotions. And let your reactions be guided by God so that you are getting the results that you will need to get and not the results of an emotional interaction or outburst of emotions. I stated to my readers to, *Do unto Others*... there was a woman who had friends that she hung out with and talked to on a regular basis. The problem was that they weren't really her friends and that the real reason why the fake friends were around her was to use her. The woman finally started to see the fake friends for who they truly were and stopped hanging with them. Sometime later she began working on a project and a true friend helped her and gave up her time for her project to succeed. The woman turned around and did to the true friend the very things that the fake friends had done to her. I wondered then why it was that we took out our hurt and disappointments on the very people who were trying to help us? It's unfair to make someone pay for what another person have done to us. It made me think, that maybe they were treated like that by the others because that's how they rolled. I realized that the principles of sowing and reaping applied to every area of our lives. Everyone has their own garden to tend. So we need to be careful how we treat people. Trust me we will reap a harvest and what that harvest will be will depend upon what we sowed. It is important that we apply the concept of sowing and reaping even in our relationships and marriages. We need to be careful that our motives are not to use our spouses. We need to have true friendship in our marriages to our spouses. And be careful not to take our hurt and disappointment out our spouses. I assure you that I speak from a place of experience. The garden of my marriage was left unkempt, and my husband and I both reaped something that we did not want to reap. We are wiser and kinder now in and to our marriage garden.

[23]Gary Chapman in *Loving Solutions: Overcoming Barriers in Your Marriage* states that, "a positive attitude can bring about change… [That] my actions are not controlled by my emotions… [It is] western society [that] has given an undue emphasis to human emotions… popular psychology has led us astray… man is more than his emotions. We experience life through the five senses: sight, sound, smell, taste, and touch. In response to what we experience through the senses, we have thoughts, feelings, desires, and actions. Feelings bears directly on our emotions. In our thoughts, we interpret what we experience through the five senses… accompanying our thoughts will be emotions… in response to these thoughts and feelings, we have desires… [And] eventually we take action based on our thoughts, emotions, and desires. We do something [that] our actions either enhance or destroy [in] relationships, our actions will affect our emotions [and] behavior [will] influence emotions. Emotions are not a firm foundation on which to build life. [It is important to] be influenced by [our] emotions, but not controlled by them. One positive action does not heal the hurt of a lifetime, but it is a step in the right direction." What I was feeling was driving my reactions to the things that I was experiencing in my marriage. I saw my husband who'd I'd married and made a real commitment with,

---
[23] Gary Chapman
Loving Solutions: Overcoming Barriers in Your Marriage 1998

separated from me and with someone who was not me, who was not his rib, who was not his wife. I heard lies from both my husband and the other women. I remembered the many years that'd we'd been married and the things that we'd shared together. I remembered the touch of our days when we were young and naïve in one another's embrace. I thought that my marriage was over, I felt something that I had never felt, I was angry and I wanted to not feel what I was feeling. I acted on my feelings and I responded to what was being presented to me. I displaced my anger, I loved my husband, I didn't deny him when he'd come to our bedroom, but I wanted my husband, I wanted my marriage. I had to come to a place during our last separation that Gary Chapman spoke about where I could "admit [that] my imperfections [didn't] mean that I [was] a failure." I was not a failure in my marriage, I did not fail my marriage. I had to reach this point so that I did not put up walls and barriers with my relationships. Chapman also stated that "walls stand as a monument to self-centered living, and it's a barrier to marital intimacy. Demolishing emotional walls is essential for rebuilding a troubled marriage. Both individual have to admit that they are imperfect and have failed each other." I failed my husband and my husband failed me. We were two imperfect people who were not completely whole, who were functioning in an institution of marriage that we'd never seen or fully experienced, operating in a role as husband and wife for which we had no point of reference. What we had was each other and a desire to be to our children what we did not experience as children. We forgot to include ourselves into that equation and lived as roommates rather than husband and wife. But this time we have a point of reference and we know to include ourselves into the equation. We live as husband and wife and not as roommates. We are to one another what we did not experience as children. Our love has stood the test and trial and remained even in the mist of the foolishness that we took one another through. I came to a place during my separation where I was as Gary Chapman stated, "no longer using [my] spouse's failures as an excuse for [my] own. This let [my] spouse know that [I was] consciously thinking about [our] marriage relationship [and] the power of love to help us in our marriage. Love is the most powerful weapons for good in the world. Love is not an emotion, love is an attitude with appropriate behavior, it affects the emotions, but it is not in itself an emotion. Love is action that grows out of thoughts. Love is the action which grows out of the attitude. Love can be learned because it is not an emotion, it is a way of thinking and behaving. The emotion of love grows out of loving actions." My husband and I were not at the point of no return, we could learn one another still and learn to love one another from one another. My husband taught me to love him unconditionally. I taught him to love me unconditionally. I loved and love him in spite of what we'd taken each other through. And we learn one another daily. Just as we fall in love daily with Jesus Christ, we are to fall in love each day with our spouses.

I had to realize that there were three versions of a truth that I was facing and not facing during our separation. My version of the truth, my husband's version of the truth and the actual truth that neither of us wanted to see. My version was everything that was wrong in my marriage and with my husband and his 'other' relationships and how I was over my husband and wanted a divorce. His version was everything that was wrong in his marriage and with me and how he'd gotten himself into 'other' situations and would have to dig himself out of these 'other' situations. And then the truth where there was trouble in our marriage because we miss-communicated with one another and didn't respond as we should have to a number of temptations that presented themselves in our marriage. I was pushing him away when I should have been drawing him closer. He was in fear of becoming his father to the point that he became his father. We've since faced our truth and learned how to communicate with one another in a way that draws us closer to one another rather than pushes us away from one another. And I have learned to pray that the Lord covers my husband and I pray more guided directed prayers when temptations present themselves in our marriage so that my husband is able to overcome those temptations. Our home is our home and our marriage is our marriage. We are not roommates and we do not live as roommates, we live as husband and wife. And where we didn't necessarily get it wrong or right with our children, we now have the opportunity to present to our grandchildren a true marriage so that they will have a point of reference from their parents and my husband and I.

Part III

Uncovered 'It'

I stand in a field of happiness remembering the ease of childhood,
That was the first time I saw you the innocence of the freedom of my imagination,
With eyes of wonderment I look up and see colors so bright and vibrant I have to smile.
I never looked for a pot of gold at the end of your colorful display,
You see I know the glory in this picture is that you allow me to see it,
Sure I am just a child, but I am one that you chose to reveal yourself to,
I look into the distance to a place that I know that you have called me to,
The portal of heaven shines through the clouds and bids me to come.
I will gladly come and see the joy that awaits me without fear of what is there,
I stay where I am because who would understand where I have gone?
I hear my name being called and that ends our time for now,
I could get use to talking to you this way because your presence is true and Strong.

Lonely with a husband and Left Uncovered

I saw that I didn't need to get used to doing things alone. My husband and I lived two separate lives. My life revolved around my church. I had to get used to living *alone* without him. I was getting into being alone. Going to concerts alone. Although my husband and I did things alone, apart from one another, it feels very different when you have to do things alone because you're separated. I wasn't alone, my youngest daughter was still living with me and I am a twin so I had never been alone, but being separated again was a different feeling of being alone.

What does it mean to be uncovered? Early on in the separation, I discovered another meaning to being uncovered. Throughout my life growing up as a teenager and early 20's I can honestly say that I didn't look at other men in any other way other than to say whether or not he was attractive or that he had a nice body or something like that, but that was as far as it went. I never desired another man. And I can remember a time when I finally came to the realization that I was attracted to one guy in particular and it threw me for a loop.

I didn't get it, I mean I understand the laws of attraction and how the world sees it, but for me this was something new and something totally out of my element and it scared me. I think I would have been okay if it was during the many times that we had separated or when we were arguing or at odds with each other, I think I could have handled it a lot better if the attraction started around one of those times, but again hind sight is 20/20 and I was literally attracted to another man for the first time of being not just married, but being with *my* husband. Even in high school I really didn't have a desire to be with anyone else or to date anyone else. So for me to have this attraction to another guy, it overwhelmed me. I can remember being so overwhelmed by it that I went to my pastor about it and I thank God for my pastor, such a wonderful man of God and he handled it and me with kid gloves because he knew that it was new to me. I think he was a little surprised by this being the first time that this had happened to me. Even though I was fairly young I was in my mid 20's when this happened, it kind of shocked him that I hadn't or didn't have this experience in my teens or early 20's of dating. I guess it was uncharacteristic for someone my age to be attracted to just one guy, not to have had more than one experience with having a boyfriend. Not saying that he thought that the teen girls would be looser, it's just common practice presumably for you to date more than one person during your high school and early college years.

 To be realistic, you don't know who you are, you're trying to find your way and you're trying to figure out what you do and don't like and every other aspect of your life. He was very encouraging and I left out of that meeting with my pastor with a new found respect for him and it was okay. This may sound crazy, but I didn't see it as okay, I thought something was wrong especially when nothing was going wrong in my marriage at that time. In my understanding it is easier for the enemy to get a foot hold in when things are going wrong in the marriage, in your relationship, but I couldn't pinpoint what it was, or whether there was anything going wrong and I just didn't realize it at the time. So when we first separated I looked back on that time and I realized that I stopped acknowledging the advances of men. I barely even spoke to another man, even if they spoke to me first. And it was just that my attention was not on them. But during this time of separation, we were not separated a year before I met a guy who I was instantly attracted to. I talked with this guy, I spent a lot of time one night with this guy. And it was more than just a physical attraction, but when I got home that night, I remember texting my husband and being so angry with him because the reality of him leaving me uncovered hit me like a sledge hammer. I could recall previous times when we were angry at each other or when I didn't want to be bothered with him or during the times that he'd leave or I'd put him out, in all of those times I never once desired another man. I don't know if in the back of my mind I knew that he'd come back, or that we would get back together as we'd always done. I don't know if that was the case or reason. I never desired another man, but this particular time I knew that this separation felt permanent. It was so different from any other time. We were definitely growing more apart, and there was a weight to *it* and had *it* been like the other separations, I would not have looked at this other guy. So in my anger I lashed out at my husband and his words were to not blame him if I wanted to have sex with someone else. And that made me angrier because that was not why I was texting him or calling him. It was the reality that another man was able to get that close to me, another man was able to awaken desires in me and it had never happened before. Even earlier when I was attracted to the other guy, it was an attraction to his looks and his conversation, but that was as far as it went because he made all kinds of advances towards me, but I didn't give it a thought because I was married and even though the marriage wasn't perfect, that didn't matter. I was going to honor my vows no matter what my husband was doing, because I can't dictate what he does, I can't lord over him. So I knew that it was all about keeping me together.

Within a year of the last separation this other man was able to pull me in instantly. He didn't have a lot of good conversation. We talked sports, basketball which I love, we had the same favorite team and I think that we spent the majority of time talking about those types of things. But it was just refreshing to talk to another man, especially a good looking one and not really dwell on the catastrophe, the desolation of my relationship with my husband. So it was after that conversation that I got home that night and I realized how important being covered really was. I use to say that we were out of order because I was the spiritual covering for my household. And I know that it is not the way that God intended, but I got caught up in it, so much so that it became my focus, my distraction for every other thing that was going on in my marriage. Every other area was lacking because I was so caught up in my being right, my spiritual walk with Christ had to be so on point because I felt that I had to cover not only my children, but I in turn had to cover my husband as well.

And it amazed me that throughout all of the time that we were together that I never looked at a man and women flirting with another partner. The man or the woman in how they could become attracted to someone else because their covering is tainted or broken or not there at all. So with my husband not being home, with my husband not being with me, it just left me wide open to the enemy. I felt like I had a bull's eye on me, I felt like I was a target. And just like the first time, that scared me. And I made up in my mind and I vowed to myself that as long as I was married, I wouldn't even engage in any type of friendship with another man. I saw how dangerous that was for me. Now sure I could have gone on and listened to what others may have said during that time. One person told me during the party, that they expected me to come back to the party with my hair messed up. This person knew that I was married and separated. I try to be conscious in all situations of not tainting my witness. To do as it says in [24]1 Thessalonians 5:22, to "abstain from all appearance of evil" and as it says in [25]Romans 14:16, to "let not then your good be evil spoken of…" and although the pain, and the frustration were still fresh, I could not let other people see me doing anything

---

[24] 1 Thessalonians 5:22
King James Bible

[25] Romans 14:16
King James Bible

other than what a good Christian woman, someone who professes and lives their love for Christ to be doing. So when that person said that to me, it was kind of like a light bulb moment. One, is this really how they saw me? Is this really how that person perceived me to be? I hadn't spent a great deal of time with that person and they didn't really know me, but just because they responded like that to me, gave me a reason to pause. It wasn't a shock to them that I left the party but that I didn't show up afterwards with my hair messed up. It was a shock to them that I had returned with my hair and clothes in place. It amazed me, and two, that this was normal in our society for a husband and wife to be separated and both parties do their own thing. I also looked at how it related to the church, because the laws of the land really didn't hold infidelity in a shameful light. As a church, we'd become so callous about separation, infidelity, and divorce. Divorce seemed just an everyday occurrence even in the church, the divorce rate is high in the church as well as in the world. In the church and the world divorce has lost its stigma, we now have divorce parties, people who remarry more than twice, and marriage itself is taken too lightly. People marry with the mindset that if it doesn't work out that they will just divorce. People don't fight for their marriages as they should. They walk away, give up or divorce.

To cheat on your spouse is a big issue, those are grounds for divorce biblically and naturally. I was then determined that no matter what was going on in my life that I would carry myself as a married woman. So even though I was uncovered in the natural and in the spirit, I had to get my mind right because it wasn't just about him, it was also about me. I learned throughout this journey so many scriptures that I never really internalized. [26]Philippians 2:12, "wherefore, my beloved, as ye have always obeyed, not as in my presence only, but now much more in my absence, work out your own salvation with fear and trembling" became a moniker for me in my everyday life. I promised myself that it didn't matter how the world does *'it,'* I had to be different. I didn't have one example in this to say what I was doing was right and that's to be commended. I had a couple of friends who never spoke ill of my husband despite his behavior. But I didn't have someone to come along side of me to encourage me in this. I had plenty who in many ways felt that I should get a divorce but they never voiced it. And those that did voice it I learned later on just how bad of a response that was to those that did. And even though I was determined to live right no matter what, my desire for companionship was not coming from my husband. So I opted for a divorce. And I warred with whether to stay married or to push for the divorce because I felt like I should be free. And I wouldn't date or talk to anyone, but as soon as I got my divorce, I would be free to date, to look for that one person that I felt that I needed that would understand me better, that one person that would put my needs ahead of their own, that would love my children even though they were adults, and respect my relationship with Christ and not hinder me or frustrate my purpose. I felt like once I received my divorce I would be ready for the next man to come into my life.

---

[26] Philippians 2:12
King James Bible

I felt that because I was uncovered that I had to do everything in my power to make sure that I did everything right because I didn't want to take anything negative or wrong that I had; and I was not putting it all on my husband because it takes two, but I was set on getting my divorce so that everything else could fall into place. I was not naïve to believe that my next relationship would be peaches and cream, but I set up in my mind that surely God had someone for me that would love me unconditionally, flaws and all with the same kind of passion and fervor that I had for them. So that was my plan, my goal. In realizing that I was uncovered and trying to adjust my lifestyle I had to deal with my children and their take on '*it*' because they were a part of '*it*', they knew the ins and outs and although we tried our best to make sure that they were not involved in any type of arguments or anything like that, our daughters knew when their dad would leave and move to other places. They were smaller when all of these things were happening and by the time they became teenager's things had to change and we as parents dealt with a lot of the teenage antics and the grandchildren way too soon. I still had to live my walk with Christ out before them to show them how '*it's*' supposed to be done. I tried to be careful not to do the preverbal male bashing when it came to their dad because that was our issue and not theirs and no matter what happened between their father and me, he was still their dad, so it was a very thin tight rope that I was walking with them. I had always been candid with my girls, I didn't give them more information than I should have. I did not believe that I should inform my girls of everything that was going on. They were not privy to a lot of things, they just remembered what they saw. My daughters, especially my youngest, found herself wanting to hook me up with somebody. Her mentality was that he was out *there* with someone else so I should be with someone else too. I understood that she lived in a world where that was okay. In her mind because I didn't verbalize to her that I was okay, that I didn't sit her down and tell her that this was right, that I didn't sit her down and put the Bible in front of her, that I wasn't okay. I didn't do all those things with her because I felt that it was none of her business. She was still a teen when her father left, so I was not going to tell her about our separation or anything that was going on between her father and me. But the reality of that was, he didn't just leave me uncovered, he left his children uncovered. And the gravity of that is still being felt. Because no matter what people say when they state that time heals all wounds, time doesn't heal all wounds only God does. After your first marriage if you have not dealt with the emotions it doesn't matter who you marry, remarry, there is not enough time that is created to heal those wombs. The Lord has to deal with each of those emotions. God is the only one who can mend a broken heart.

It was as [27]Gary Chapman stated in *Loving Solutions: Overcoming Barriers in Your Marriage,* "when parents' divorce, children lose something that is fundamental to their development: the family structure. Children feel rejected, children get angry." My daughter went out of control in her high school year to the point that we didn't

---

[27] Gary Chapman
Loving Solutions: Overcoming Barriers in Your Marriage

believe that she would graduate. I could have easily taken the route that others had taken that she'll be alright in the long run, she'll get over *'it'* in the long run. I couldn't because *'it'* was so in my face, I had to deal with *'it'*, her struggles with *'it'*, she never internalized that it was my mom and dad that were separated, she always stated that her dad left her. I think towards the end when she was about to graduate she had to work harder, because the separation had defined who she was, she lost her desire and will to be effective, she was drowning in depression and did not know it. She started to rephrase *'it'* and state that when my dad left me and my mom. So I had to forget about me, and make sure that my daughter was okay. I couldn't heal her hurt, but I could let her know that I understood her hurt. So as we were dealing with that and getting over that, my daughter wanted to hook me up with just anyone that she felt I would like. I had to sit her down and explain to her what I felt a real woman does, in that a real woman doesn't react because of what others have done to them. She wanted to see me happy. It dawned on me that she didn't think that I was happy. By that time, we were two years into the separation. I couldn't say that I looked like someone that was happy before our conversation. I told her that I was as happy that I could be in the situation that I was in and I was very clear to her that as a young woman, that having a man just to have a man did not make you happy. If you are not happy before you allow someone into your life, then you never will be happy.

I had to explain to her that her happiness is her own responsibility and no one else's. She had to know that her happiness did not lie in her having a mate. That it didn't matter what her dad was doing, we don't know what he's doing, and we don't place judgment or assume anything. I needed her to understand that my life was not revolving around what somebody else did, neither was it going to stop if I got someone else as a companion. Above anything else that I thought, felt, or did, I had to do the will of God concerning my life. That was the most important thing that I wanted her to understand. I was still married to her father and I was not entering any male friendships, dates, and so forth. And until God gave me a revelation into what was going on in my marriage that was what it was going to be. She understood and didn't understand at the same time. She felt that it was unfair and that to her, I was stuck in limbo. It wasn't just my daughter that felt that way either, others that were in my life felt that way, and at times I even felt that way. So dealing with being uncovered was the most trying time during the separation, but the most rewarding because I learned so many biblical principles throughout this and the true role of the male and female in a family unit, relationship, and marriage. And that it is a no win situation when it is just me doing it and not me and my spouse. I learned how to pray more and in a different way throughout this, and how to make sure that my children were taken care of emotionally. It's through this separation that I learned to trust God even when I couldn't trace Him.

I live my life by three main points now, one to be Christ minded and Kingdom focused at all times, two to trust God even when I can't trace Him, and the third thing is that I am not where I want to be, but I am exactly where God has me. I don't have any doubt no matter what I am feeling or going through, I am exactly where God has me. It is an awesome feeling. To understand that when I don't have the covering from my husband, that God will be my covering in addition to my Pastor and First Lady. There is no better reward than to serve God's under Sheppard. Walking through this and learning these lessons and being uncovered, I think that I was uncovered to be covered. It may not make sense, but everything that happened in my life, either God ordained it, or He allowed it. And I know that He did not ordain the separation, that was on the part of me and my husband but He allowed it. Satan is at the throne of God daily petitioning to do whatever to me and to my marriage. I know that I already have the victory. God would not allow it if I wasn't going to come out victorious.

In my desiring a divorce, I realized that it was from an emotional place. I wanted to be free from what I was experiencing with my husband during our last separation. But I honored the vows that I spoke on our wedding day and my spiritual belief and what I have come to know about my God, I was discouraged from getting a divorce. I had to confront the situation. I had to confront through prayer the attack that was on my husband, myself, and our marriage. The only way to do this was to come out of my emotional place. My husband was not my enemy. The devil is my enemy. The devil has been trying to destroy the institution of marriage and the family unit since Adam and Eve. I had to shift my thinking from what I was experiencing with my husband to what the enemy was doing through my husband to and in our marriage.

Protect your Core

Your ribs protect the chest cavity within the body. The chest cavity is where major organs are encased such as your lungs and your heart.[28] Health line states that,

The rib cage is collectively made up of long, curved individual bones with joint-connections to the spinal vertebrae. At the chest, many rib bones connect to the sternum via costal cartilage, segments of hyaline cartilage that allow the rib cage to expand during respiration. Although fixed into place, these ribs do allow for some outward movement, and this helps stabilize the chest during inhalation and exhalation.

The human rib cage is made up of 12 paired rib bones; each are symmetrically paired on a right and left side. Of all 24 ribs, the first seven pairs are often labeled as "true." These bones are connected to the costal cartilage while the five other "false" sets are not. Three of those connected to the non-costal cartilage, and two are deemed to be "floating" which means they only connect to the spine.

---

[28] Health line http://www.healthline.com/human-body-maps/ribs

So in essence, your rib cage protects your core. When I was dealing with the emotions of being left uncovered, I had to think and put myself on the other side if you will and ask that if the rib cage protects the chest cavity, which in turn protects vital organs, in particular the heart, then when a rib is dislocated, what did that do? In my particular case I answered that it left the heart vulnerable. Except that a dislocated rib according to [29]Hub Pages and generally all medical sites,

Is a rib bone that has been disconnected from the spine or breastbone. [And] if left untreated, the dislocated rib may damage nearby blood vessels, nerves, and or ligaments.

The area becomes vulnerable to trauma, stems from weakness and causes severe pain. It would be easy for one to just be selfish in their thinking to believe that the protection from the rib cage is one sided as we often do, but the bottom line is that when a rib is dislocated within/from the rib cage and by rib, and by rib I mean a wife, there is a lack of protection, an increase in vulnerability or trauma, and severe pain. Both the husband and the wife go through something when a rib is dislocated within/from the rib cage. [30]Genesis 2:7-9, 15-23, 25

And the Lord God formed man of the dust of the ground and breathed into his nostrils the breath of life; and man became a living

---

[29] Hub Pages
Heal Dove
https://healdove.com/injuries/A-Complete-Guide-to-Dislocated-Ribs-Symptoms-Treatment-and-Causes

[30] Genesis 2:7-9, 15-23, 25
King James Bible

soul. And the Lord God planted a garden eastward in Eden: and there he put the man whom he had formed. And out of the ground made the Lord God to grow every tree that is pleasant to the sight, and good for food; the tree of life also in the midst of the garden, and the tree of knowledge of good and evil. And the Lord God took the man and put him into the Garden of Eden **to dress it and to keep it.** *And the Lord God commanded the man, saying of every tree of the garden thou may freely eat: But of the tree of knowledge of good and evil, thou shall not eat of it: for in the day that thou eat thereof thou shalt surely die. And the Lord God said that it is not good that man should be alone. I will make him a help meet for him. And out of the ground the Lord God formed every beast of the field and every fowl of the air; and brought them to Adam to see what he would call them: and whatsoever Adam called every living creature that was the name thereof. Adam gave names to all cattle, and to the fowls of the air, and to every beast of the field: but for Adam there was not found a help meet for him. And the Lord caused a deep sleep to fall upon Adam, and he slept: and he took one of his ribs, and closed up the flesh instead thereof; and the rib which the Lord God had taken from the man, made him a woman, and brought her unto the man. And Adam said, this is now bone of my bones and flesh of my flesh: she shall be called Woman, because she was taken out of Man. And they were both naked, the man and his wife, and not ashamed.*

    I had a discussion about the scriptures or the account in the Bible concerning Adam and Eve particularly when they'd eaten of the tree of the knowledge of good and evil. And the consequences of those actions.[31]Genesis 3:1-7,

Now the serpent was more subtle that any beast of the field which the Lord God had made. And he said unto the woman, Yea, hath God said ye shall not eat of every tree of the garden? And the woman said unto the serpent, we may eat of the fruit of the trees of the garden: But of the fruit of the tree which is in the midst of the garden, God hath said ye shall not eat of it, neither shall ye touch it least ye die. And the serpent said unto the woman, ye shall not surely die. For God doth know that in the day ye eat thereof, then your eyes shall be opened and ye shall be as gods, knowing good and evil. And when the woman saw that the tree was good for food, and that it was pleasant to the eyes and a tree to be desired to make one wise, she took of the fruit thereof and did eat, and gave also unto her husband with her and he did eat. And the eyes of them both were opened and they knew that they were naked; and they sewed fig leaves together, and made themselves aprons.

Adam and Eve had become aware of themselves being naked and covered themselves.[32]Genesis 3:9-21

And the Lord God called unto Adam, and said unto him, where art thou? And he said, I heard thy voice in the garden, and I was afraid, because I was naked; and I hid myself. And He said, who told thee that thou was naked? Hast thou eaten of the tree, whereof

---

[31] Genesis 3:1-7
King James Bible

[32] Genesis 3:9-21
King James Bible

*I commanded thee that thou shouldest not eat? And the man said, the woman thou gavest to be with me, she gave me of the tree, and I did eat. And the Lord God said unto the woman, what is this that thou hast done? And the woman said, the serpent beguiled me, and I did eat. And the Lord God said unto the serpent, Because thou hast done this, thou art cursed above all cattle, and above every beast of the field; upon thy belly shalt thou go, and dust shalt thou eat all the days of thy life: And **I will put enmity between thee and the woman, and between thy seed and her seed; it shall bruise thy head, and thou shalt bruise her heel.** Unto the woman he said, I will greatly multiply thy sorrow and thy conception; in sorrow thou shalt bring forth children; and **thy desire shall be to thy husband**, and he shall rule over thee. And unto Adam he said, Because thou hast hearkened unto the voice of thy wife, and hast eaten of the tree, of which I commanded thee, saying, Thou shalt not eat of it: cursed is the ground for thy sake; in sorrow shalt thou eat of it all the days of thy life; Thorns also and thistles shall it bring forth to thee; and thou shalt eat the herb of the field; In the sweat of thy face shalt thou eat bread, till thou return unto the ground; for out of it was thou taken: for dust thou art, and unto dust shalt thou return. And **Adam called his wife's mane Eve**; because she was the mother of all living. Unto Adam also to his wife did the Lord God make coats of skins, and clothed them.*

The consequences or the curse started with the serpent, next the woman, and lastly Adam. The serpent would have to crawl on its belly and experience always enmity between the women, hers and its seed (children) for the woman would bruise the head of the serpent and the serpent would bruise the heel of the woman's feet. In addition, the woman's sorrow was increased in the conception and the birth of her children, her desires would be for her husband, and that he would have rule over her. For Adam it was going to be hard for him to take care of himself, his wife, his family because the Lord cursed the ground making it a hard labor to till. It was even more interesting to me that in pain or sorrow Eve would conceive and birth children, and that her heart would be forever turned towards the man. It's open to interpretation as to what that exactly means, but I'd experienced it as a woman. In my teenage years, I'd gotten pregnant with my hymen in place which meant that upon delivery my hymen was broken. The delivery room, the process of giving birth can bring about a death to both the mother and the baby. I'd married young and I was and am constantly experiencing enmity with the enemy. I have to constantly pray over my children and my husband as I maintain within our household.

Going through the last separation, I wondered about the love and the commitment that some of us had as women, as wives towards our husband's. It often at times seemed and felt like a curse and I thought about Eve and how it seemed that no matter what the man did, there were quite a few of us who continued to forgive our husband's and stayed in our marriages. I know that I am a firm believer in forgiveness so that God can forgive me as it states in [33]Matthew 6:14-15,

---

[33] Matthew 6:14-15
King James Bible

"For if ye forgive men their trespasses, your heavenly Father will also forgive you; But if ye forgive not men their trespasses, neither will your Father forgive your trespasses." I thought about my growing up before I came of age and came to a knowledge of who God is and how my relationship began to grow. I can't say that I was always in line to forgive my husband because God said so. There were plenty of times that I would forgive him simply because I loved him, I couldn't imagine my life without him. My heart forever turned towards my husband. Of course it looks good and it sounds good to say that I am going to forgive him because God says that we ought to forgive. In reality however that wasn't exactly the case. It had been set for me by the Lord God Himself that as a wife my heart would be forever towards my husband. I started thinking more and more on how the last separation and my being misplaced affected my husband. Any woman that has been in love can attest to the fact that we as women protect our men emotionally from a number of things. I was thinking about how men don't always understand us and how we don't always understand them, but that women do a number of things in the relationship to make sure that the man is protected emotionally. And I don't want to get into the whole discussion about the double standard between men and women where men are almost always celebrated for being promiscuous whereas women are deemed a whore or a slut. Or how we respond and function in the world, but any woman can attest to the fact that if you really love him, as a woman you would do everything in your power to protect him emotionally. The vast majority of men don't deal directly with feelings, some would rather bottle their feelings up or suppress their feelings and act as if their feelings do not exist. And for most women it is dominant within us to deal with feelings or matters of the heart so we can pretty much gaze at our husbands and know what will be okay or what will destroy him emotionally. As women we also protect our husbands from information. I've heard women say that they would never tell their husband if they cheated, men generally get caught, but women feel that their husbands wouldn't be able to handle that type of information if the woman told her husband that she'd cheated. The music group TLC have a song entitled *"Creep"* and two of the lines in the lyrics says that "if he knew the things I did, he couldn't handle me. And I choose to keep him protected, oh. "He wouldn't be able to handle knowing that she was doing the same thing that he was doing. This is the double standard, so as women we often take on the role of making sure that we protect their heart in that their heart is not damaged. Unfortunately, we forget that while trying to make sure that no one else damages their heart that we as the wives do much of the damaging.

There was a time when I was working as a bus operator and I hadn't been at the job longer than a year before I would be tested in this area. I had to take a training course for safety and there was this one particular guy who I found that I had a lot in common with, he was married as well, and he had the same number of children. He and I had a lot to talk about during training breaks. I am generally a people person, so by me being so friendly sometimes it left me vulnerable to preying men. I didn't do anything wrong, I didn't flirt, however, he became a bit aggressive in trying to talk to me even though we were both married. I remember on one occasion after training I was in the process of making a relief, this is where you relieve one driver to resume the route of the bus and as I was making my relief, he got on the bus. I asked him if he had to work that day but he stated that he was off that day and that he'd decided that he would ride the bus with me. I was nervous about that because in my mind I thought who does that. He had a wife and children at home and he wanted to ride the bus with me while I was working. I made it a point that I would set him straight. I told him that if I maybe did something that I didn't know unconsciously in misleading him into thinking that I would date him or have a fling with him or would have an affair I apologize. I couldn't recall any conversations where I said or lead on to any of those things or had done anything to make him believe or think that that was something that I would have wanted. I remember telling him that the mere fact that I was having that conversation with him would hurt my husband and I didn't want to do that. Even though there wasn't anything going on, but because another married man was trying to hit on me it was bothering me to no end and I knew what that type of situation or information would do to my husband emotionally.

Of course hindsight is 20/20 and most of the time if someone is accusing you of doing something so strongly, it is because they are doing the very thing that they are accusing you of. And as I look back on it, that probably was the case with my husband, but I have never been the type to do two wrongs, because two wrongs don't make things right. And that's just one of the ways that as a woman, as a wife I always stayed on guard to protect my husband, to protect his heart. In the case of bad information, we'll get the information and then try to figure out the best way to tell our husband's that would cause the least harm and often times we'll omit certain things to protect them. Sometimes that back fires to our detriment so I found myself having a light bulb moment in the situation with my coworker. Information that I thought at the time was unnecessary and at the same time may have hurt him, I failed to speak up about certain details, certain things all because I believed that I was in protection mode. And when you are dealing with situations where there is infidelity or mistrust your good will turn out to be evil spoken of by your spouse because once you are in the thick of arguments, disagreements, or heading for a divorce, things are always magnified. Neither of you will trust the other, and nothing that is said will be believed, and it is a vicious cycle that the enemy keeps active until he reaches the ultimate goal of the destruction of the family unit and a desolation of your marriage.

For that is what the enemy is after. He wants to destroy the family unit. He began in the Garden of Eden by persuading and deceiving Eve and he has been after marriages ever since. Marriages represent oneness, order, and brings about procreation. A wife is a help meet. A husband is a provider and a covering to his household. Remember Adam was created to "dress and keep" the garden. This is the perfect union that the Lord stands for in which He states in [34]Matthew

---

[34] Matthew 19:5-6
King James Bible

19:5-6, "... for this cause shall a man leave father and mother, and shall cleave to his wife: and they twain shall be one flesh? Wherefore they are no more twain, but one flesh. What therefore God hath joined together, let no man put asunder. "The man and the woman are no longer two, but one. So then with me being separated there were times when I thought about what others were doing to him and that sounded and felt crazy, but I felt like he was my child in a since and out of what I believed to be my fierce dedication to him, I had to protect him from being hurt. I wondered about the relationships that he was in, just because I chose not to engage in any relationships until my fictional divorce did not mean that he was doing the same. So there was always this thought in the back of my mind where I was hoping or thinking or praying that whomever the woman/women were that they would not damage his heart any further than it already had been damaged. And the reality is that we can't protect our spouse totally emotionally. Something's are out of our hand and that doesn't mean that the desire to be there to protect his heart stops, it just means that I could not protect him emotionally from everything. Even though throughout the separation and wanting a divorce many times we are the ones inflicting the damage upon our husband's heart. It is almost as if we are saying that if anyone is going to do it, it's going to be 'me' and not someone else. You become possessive. You don't even realize how strong the marital covenant is even when neither of you are abiding by it. The Bible says that the two shall become one flesh and you take on the responsibility of protecting what has been entrusted to you. And it seems almost primitive in nature. If a man says that his wife is his, she may as an independent strong woman say that he doesn't own her, but in actuality he does and vice versa because the two shall become one. I use to hear that all of the time and I struggle even now with that statement, that reality because in my flesh dwells no good thing and asking me to be submissive was like you've cursed/used foul language towards me. I rationalized that he was not doing what he was supposed to do as a husband so why should I have to succumb or acquiesce. Why did I have to become a submissive wife?

It didn't matter what he did or didn't do, I only had control over me. And in reality I didn't even have that because the Lord has control over me. There were days that I wanted to call him up and ask him how he was doing because on those days I felt a void. Even on the days that I was happy, I felt a void, I felt like I was supposed to be doing something that I was supposed to be somewhere. And it had nothing to do with a missed appointment or anything else and it was not mental at all, but it was all a matter of my heart and my forever desire towards my husband. In how deep it really is for two people to come together in marriage and become one, and how I felt certain things as a result that I was sure of whatever he was feeling or going through at those particular times when I wanted to reach out to him, when I felt the void. And I knew that if we were still together I would be able to do my *job* as his wife and guard his heart. He is my soul mate and we are joined together as one and where I felt a void, he felt a void because we were not in place, we were not where we should have been as husband and wife. And the void is a curse and a blessing because my desire is forever towards my husband. And my vow to be his wife is forever towards my husband and our marriage. I felt a void because I as his rib was out of place so I was not functioning as I should have been functioning within our marriage and family unit. I was displaced, I was dislocated.

The chest cavity protects the lungs, the very area that I believe sustains life. For once your oxygen is cut off, you are not able to breath, and the necessary amount of oxygen to stay alive does not go to the heart or to the brain. What an important task then, the responsibility that your ribs take on protecting the chest cavity that protects the heart and lungs. So much so that if I don't protect, if I'm misplaced or if I've left the area opened and vulnerable to the attack of the enemy, and if I am out of place then another woman can come in and take his breath away. Which would then cause oxygen to be missing from the brain to the point that he could not make the appropriate decisions. I wanted to know how much damage was done as a result of someone else, another woman having taken his breath away. The enemy was only able to use her because I was displaced, dislocated, not in the place that I should have been in. I was not in my praying position when I left him open and vulnerable to the attack of the enemy. I was not in my submissive role. Maybe my words to someone else at the moment were negative, maybe I wasn't speaking life into my marriage or into my husband, maybe I didn't care enough about my situation. Maybe I was being selfish and only thinking of myself. My dislocation caused a hole for his heart and his lung to be exposed. I didn't protect the core, his core.

How could I do that if I was dislocated? How was that possible if I was dislocated? When you are dislocated you are not in the area that you should be. And I am not one to say that I placed all of the blame on myself either. Often times when I had these types of discussions it was always stated to me that I was making excuses for him or for her. And for me it was not about making excuses, it was about taking responsibility for the part that I played in the relationship, in my marriage. It took two, and I think that that is the biggest issue in most couple's divorces that by the time he and she realize that they have been so compromised they feel like it's too late. By the time she realizes that she is dislocated he's already gone and by the time he realizes that he has a dislocation he's too far gone in another situation. Your ribs protect your core and your core is where you find stability. Your chest cavity protects the vital organs that are responsible for pumping blood and oxygen throughout your body. So your rib and your chest cavity have to be protected at all times. Remember, a dislocated rib according to Hub Pages and generally every medical site "is a rib bone that has been disconnected from the spine or breastbone… [And] if left untreated, the dislocated rib may damage nearby blood vessels, nerves, and/or ligaments." The area becomes vulnerable to trauma, stems from weakness and causes severe pain. For my marriage, I had been disconnected from the oneness and the covering. My husband was left vulnerable to the enemy, I was left vulnerable to the enemy, my household, our children, our finances, and our marriage was left vulnerable to the enemy. Every area became damaged by and to trauma. I was weak, my husband was weak. And our whole family unit was in pain. In [35]Proverbs 4:23 the scripture says to "keep thy heart with all diligence, for out of it are the issues of life." Not taking on the full responsibility of making sure that my husband's heart was not damaged, but that as a wife assuming my role and doing what God put my husband and me together to do. We both had a role to play to uphold this union. It is not your responsibility to take care of the sole emotional stability of your spouse, only God can do that, but it is your responsibility as a wife to make sure that your husband is emotionally okay. Your life holds weight in your spouse's life and any other way of thinking is immature. You have to do what needs to be done to protect those vulnerable areas. And for the man who realizes that his rib is dislocated, it is up to him to get the help that he needs to have that rib, his wife put back into place and to not let guilt or shame get in the way of doing so. You have to protect your core at all times. For the man who doesn't know this will always engage in activities that will have his rib dislocated.

---

[35] Proverbs 4:23
King James Bible

Part IV

When do I get to be me? When can I just lay out the person I know for other to see? You know the real me,
The me who sees the sunset in the sunrise and shares a joyous laugh,
Because I know a secret that is between me and the horizon,
We share a bond that others never see,
For every day that starts will end in the same way for me,
I'm stuck in the middle of a great chasm so wide there is enough room for my thoughts and all of the people I want to drag with me into my world,
A world where I get to be me, the real me.
The me that feels so deeply for everyone that I love and even those I think I hate,
Everybody understands me here and I am not judged I am just loved,
Not just any kind of love but an unconditional and pure love,
In my world I'm not forced to put on a mask to hide the hurt and the pain that I live, with and wear like a second skin. My world allows crying and screaming without fear,
You see in my world I'm free to be me, to dance sing be happy and carefree.
To love and give of myself uninhibited,
In my world I can be the real me not just what people think and see.

You have to be whole

I started thinking about [36]Mark 10:8, "and the two will become one flesh. So they are no longer two, but one flesh." In how the two individually come into the relationship with their own ideas and their own way of thinking. Each come into the relationship being a product of their own environment in how they were raised. And even though some people are similar in temperament and in how they see things. More often than not you grow up learning different things from your family traits. I then started thinking about all of the things that made me who I am, how my childhood effected the way that I see things as an adult, and how important it is for the two individually to be whole before they come into any relationship. Not perfect, but whole in mind and in spirit. Take an orange for example, if you have half of an orange there is nothing that you can do to make that half of an orange a whole orange when it started off as a half of an orange. Whereas if I had a whole orange, I could take

---

[36] Mark 10:8
King James Bible

that whole orange and break it in half as well as put it together and it would still be a whole orange. But a half of orange, if I break that up, it becomes quarters of an orange. You have to be whole before you can be a half or part of a relationship.

That revelation came to me during one of my discussions that I had with my husband in our home during the time of our last separation. And when I said that to him he had this perplexed look upon his face. To be honest, I didn't really hear what I said or understood what I said until after he left the house. I started to think about it, his response, and why he responded that way. I thought about all of the different things that had happened to him in his childhood, teen years, and young adult years; and I realized that as young as we were when we started dating, a lot had happened in our lives before we'd even met. It seemed typical, our upbringing, but it really wasn't, realizing that we had issues and things that needed to be settled before we entered into our relationship. If they were not settled, they were going to show up in our relationship and unfortunately, like a lot of us, we didn't know or were aware that certain things in our childhood affected the way that we saw things. Example, I didn't grow up with a father in the house, my mother was a single parent who took care of five children on her own. She did the best that she could despite her circumstances. This was mid to late 60's early 70's and I was growing up with four other siblings in a house where there were just certain things that I didn't get to experience or that I didn't get the opportunity to learn from. There were things that happened in my childhood that were normal for me, but then as I grew older I realized that they weren't so normal. There were many things in my childhood that affected the way that I saw things. I didn't have the role model that I could pattern my marriage after. I'd knew of married couples and my mother had friends that were married, but I didn't see intimate details in how they functioned as a married couple. I did however get to see how single mothers lived. My family lived in a building that was filled with single mothers and children. There were a handful of married couples, single men, and those who cohabitated. I saw more of what was the perceived norm for our society than what God intended for me to experience and that affected me in my relationships.

When times were hard in my marriage, or when I got confused about certain things, who I was as it related to my marriage, I didn't have anything to go on. It wasn't like I could ask advice from my mother, she married, but had been separated for years. There were my godparents, who were good to me, and I call my godfather my dad. I know of my biological father I don't have a good relationship with him. I didn't spend the majority of my time at my godparents, but when I did go to their home, I got to see what should have been the family unit that every child deserves; but because I didn't see that and the single parenting experience was the norm, I didn't think anything of it. So when times were rough in my marriage with my husband, especially earlier on in our marriage when we would separate and my husband would leave or I would put him out, that was normal to me. I knew in my heart that it should not have been that way, but I was so focused on being able to do it on my own, or to do it all myself because that was what I saw. It was like I had to do it, I had to be strong enough to take care of my children with or without my husband. And it should not have been a choice, it should have been to keep the family unit together. I'm not one of those that advocate for abuse, I am one who now sees the value of children growing up in the home with their fathers. I am not a man I cannot even begin to think like a man. I could not teach our daughters from a male perspective, that is what their dad was for and while some father's come and go, the bottom line is that there is something to be said for children going to bed knowing the security that both of their parents are there and waking up in the morning and knowing that they have both of their parents who are loving them and taking care of them and making sure that they are okay and that they are provided for. As a woman, a black woman, the stigma holds strong that we are the strong women who have to take care of ourselves no matter what and in turn we push the man away. It is like it is a perpetual cycle that some of us do not know how to get out of. So whenever I would have problems in my marriage I would bail, I did not like confrontation because of where it took me or made me feel. I could not separate the anger, hurt or disappointment in my marriage, it all manifested as anger and frustration of not being able to get it right or to get him to understand what I was thinking, saying or feeling. So I didn't know who I was.

 A friend and I would say the different facades or personalities for women and who we are and how some of us don't know who we are as a wife. Partly because that part of who we are as a wife

You have to be whole

hadn't manifested because we hadn't been married. For me I knew who I was as a sister, as a daughter, but I did not know who I was as myself. I began to learn. Growing up I had never been alone, I had my siblings, and I am a twin so I didn't even have the womb alone. By the time that I'd gotten my own room, my oldest daughter was born and I shared the room with her. I didn't get the opportunity to experience being alone. I didn't even go away for college. I had two children by the time I graduated from high school, my mindset was to be a homebody and to take care of my children and husband, then boyfriend. I was not whole, I was fragmented in every area. I was not capable or mature enough to continue growing up taking care of children and being a wife. I didn't know who I was before I became a mother and a wife. I found out as I learned who I am as a mother. I am still finding out or learning who I am as a wife because I'd never functioned as a wife. My husband was my friend. We grew up together, we were children raising children. By the time I was eighteen I'd moved into my own apartment and assumed the full responsibility for providing for myself and my daughters. I had to learn as I went along and at the same time learn who I was. I was trying to live a Godly life as well and find my way through all that I was experiencing.

I've since learned through [37]Gary Chapman in *Loving Solutions: Overcoming Barriers in Your Marriage* that there are "four types of personality (the hidden self) [which has] patterned [our] way

---

[37] Gary Chapman
Loving Solutions: Overcoming Barriers in Your Marriage

of responding to life [which] greatly impacts behavior. One, the peacemaker: calm, slow, easy-going, well-balanced personality, typically pleasant, doesn't like conflicts, seldom seems ruffled, and rarely expresses anger, has emotions, but does not easily reveal them. Two, the controller: the quick, active, practical, strong-willed person, self-sufficient, independent, decisive, and opinionated, thrives on activity, problems are seen as challenges. Three, the care taker: self-sacrificing, gifted perfectionist who wants to meet the needs of others, emotional nature is extremely sensitive, extremely dependable, and has high standards for oneself and others, exceptional analytical abilities, finds their greatest meaning in life through personal sacrifice and service to others, fail to recognize their own emotional needs. Four, the party maker: the warm, lively, excited personality, life is a party, enjoys people, does not like solitude, the life of the party never at a loss for words, come across as undependable and undisciplined. We are attracted to those who have strengths in the areas where we are weak. [In] understanding personality patterns, we tend to seek to meet ones psychological and spiritual needs in keeping with one's personality. The methods used to satisfy hidden needs will be influenced by our personality. We are influenced, not controlled by your personality.[And] you [will need to] take the better way even if it takes you out of your comfort zone. [And then there is] the irresponsible spouse [whose] efforts compounded the problem [where one would need to] clarify the problem. [Finding still that] one's perception of reality is always colored by our own personality, values, and desires."

You have to be whole

The emotional wear and tear of a marriage can be very dangerous and catastrophic in certain areas when you are not whole, or when you have too many fragmented pieces of yourself where some of the pieces you don't even know where they are and others you don't even know where they fit into your life. Fragmented trying to sustain a marriage where your focus has to be on your spouse, trying to understand and come to terms with them as number one. I could not reconcile that and then as a strong "black woman" learning how to take my hands off of things, stepping back, and allowing my husband to be the man, to be the head. This is what I mean by my child hood, the fragments of my child hood that tainted my adulthood with me growing up and not being able to get away from those ideals. And as much as I missed my husband when we'd separate throughout our marriage, I went on with my life. I didn't press upon him to do anything, to take care of me or our daughters. I wanted nothing from him even when he tried to help. It didn't even enter my mind to ask him for anything, I dreaded asking him for anything, and who does that? In therapy, I realized all of these things, some of it came through divine revelation, God opened my eyes about it and I just thought at one point in time, wow, all the things that I'd been going through, all of the things that manifested in my life were as a result of the things that I'd gone through as a child. I thought about all of those things, I thought about my spouse, and it was like wow, of course our stories are different, but at the same time if I was dealing with all of the things that I was dealing with, I couldn't even imagine what he was dealing with. Men and women are different in the way that we see and process things. I thought, man how could we sustain a marriage, living like that, not addressing our issues, not getting to the root of our problems. Marriages don't just up and end, these were things that were in the back of my mind for so long and I struggled with it in silence. I didn't even tell my closest friend the depth of my disappointment or my pain. I couldn't share with friends because I didn't have a clue as to how to express what I was feeling and experiencing, everything was new, everything was raw, and my emotions were haywire.

Even with everything that was going on, as a result of how I was raised, I put me on the back burner and dealt with everybody else, making sure my children were okay. I still had to make sure that my children were okay and that they were not affected by what was going on. I couldn't even invest in me. Getting myself whole, then and now looking back on my marriage, I always would think about my marriage, in that if I had it to do all over again, I wondered would I? Would I marry him? If I knew then what I know now, would I have married my husband? The answer would be yes and no, and not because of the pain that I'd gone through with the separation, the confusion, the frustration, the feeling of inadequacy, and unworthiness. I could overcome these feelings, because I could forgive. No, I wouldn't marry my husband at the time that I did. I wasn't whole and neither was he. I would have waited to marry him. I love him, life for me was with him, and I spent half my life with him.

Understanding that one must be whole before they can be a half of anything is the best advice that I could offer someone. "Everyone has baggage, find someone who will help you unpack" I can agree with that in part, no one is perfect, no one is 100% starting out, but if you can meet someone and be at least 80% then that is a start. I'd recently read a meme by a woman who refers to herself as the [38]*The Great Kamryn* that, "the truth is that the more intimately you know someone, the more clearly you'll see their flaws. That's just the way it is. This is why marriages fail, why children are abandoned, why friendships don't last. You might think you love someone until you see the way they act when they're out of money or under pressure or hungry, for goodness' sake. Love is something different. Love is choosing to serve someone and be with someone in spite of their filthy heart. Love is patient and kind, love is deliberate. Love is hard. Love is pain and sacrifice, it's seeing the darkness in another person and defying the impulse to jump ship." The reality is that we are all human, when you love someone, you don't see their faults or flaws, but when their uncovered to you, their flaws, how they respond to various things, that is when love really shows up and you understand what real love is and you don't walk out.

Understanding and accepting that people come to you flawed, fragmented, and taking them for who they are, and deciding, making a conscious choice to love them is the first step to me, to being whole. This is the greatest gift that you can give anybody. I thought about how I am looked upon, how I am seen and I realized that I no longer care. This journey has been hard and rough, I know who I am now. I

---

[38] The Great Kamryn
http://www.goodreads.com/quotes/960187-the-truth-is-that-the-more-intimately-you-know-someone

A Dislocated Rib

am a whole person now. My happiness starts with me. I am thankful for this experience of being dislocated from my life mate, my husband.[39] Gary Chapman in *Loving Solutions: Overcoming Barriers in Your Marriage* helped me to see that "husbands and wives speak different love languages, [that there are] five basic languages of love. [One,] words of affirmation: verbally affirming them for the good things they do. [Two,] quality time: giving them your undivided attention. [Three,] receiving gifts. [Four] acts of service: doing things for your spouse, anything that you know is meaningful to him/her. [Five,] physical touch. When you choose to reach out with a loving attitude and loving actions toward your spouse in spite of past failures you are creating a climate where conflicts can be resolved, wrongs can confessed, and a marriage can be reborn. I am responsible for my own attitude. Attitude affects action. I cannot change others, but I can influence others. My actions are not controlled by my emotions. [And] admitting my imperfections does not mean that I am a failure." I understand now and accept my husband for where he is and I've learned to communicate with him using his love language and vice versa.

I now have a strong passion for marriages and a desire to see them whole, and for families to be intact. I would love nothing more than for God to get the victory in every marriage that I pray for so that the enemy won't win and tear up another family. No matter what I went through, I can encourage someone to stay in

---

[39] Gary Chapman
Loving Solutions: Overcoming Barriers in Your Marriage

You have to be whole

their marriage. [40]Matthew 19:6, "Therefore they are no longer twain, but one flesh. What therefore God hath joined together, let not man put asunder." And not just outside forces, but no one. A marriage contract is a covenant. I feel honored to have gone through this experience, God trusted me to go through this, and He was with me every step of the way. I am not weak or gullible for not divorcing my husband. [41]Matthew 5:44, "But I say unto you, Love your enemies, bless them that curse you, do good to them that hate you, and pray for them which despitefully use you, and persecute you;". I can't just take vengeance on and want to get back at my husband. [42]Romans 12:9, "Dearly beloved, avenge not yourselves, but rather give place unto wrath: for it is written, Vengeance is mine; I will repay, saith the Lord." And if you go deeper, God forgives us all of the time, [43]Romans 3:23, "for all have sinned, and come short of the glory of God;" We should extend grace to our spouses who have hurt us. [44]Ephesians 4:16, "From whom the whole body fitly joined together and compacted by that which every joint supplieth, according to the effectual working in the measure of every part,

---

[40] Matthew 19:6
King James Bible

[41] Matthew 5:44
King James Bible

[42] Romans 12:9
King James Bible

[43] Romans 3:23
King James Bible

[44] Ephesians 4:16
King James Bible

maketh increase of the body unto the edifying of itself in love." [45]1 Peter 4:8, "And above all things have fervent charity among yourselves: for charity shall cover the multitude of sins." I've learned through prayer, therapy, divine revelation and [46]Gary Chapman in *Loving Solutions: Overcoming Barriers in Your Marriage* that in a marriage, in my marriage, it was important that my husband and I "balance out [our] ambitions so that every area in [our] relationship [was] covered. [We do this by] analyzing the source of the problem, [which is most often] the past, [our] parents, [and asking the hard questions such as] is he following the model of his father, is he rebelling against the model of his father, [because] all of us are influenced by the model of our parents. Many of us are keenly aware of our parents' failures (the voice of the non-parent), some of us consciously or subconsciously trying hard to be different. [My husband and I] did not want to repeat the mistakes of our parents [however] often those efforts lead us to other extremes.[We found that] much of [our] behavior is motivated by [our] inner emotional needs. [So that it is important to] take positive action because once again, [I nor my husband] cannot control [one another's] behavior, [only God can do that], but [we] can influence [one another] through positive actions even while [our] emotions are negative. [That it is important to always] admit [our] mistakes, [to develop a plan and see it all the way through] slow, steady change, give suggestions

---

[45] 1 Peter 4:8
King James Bible

[46] Gary Chapman
Loving Solutions: Overcoming Barriers in Your Marriage

to [one another], make constructive changes, an understanding of [my husband's] inner needs and a willingness to change [my] own behavior [brought] about a positive change. Asking forgiveness, using though love, love sometimes must be hard and firm, [because] if you really care about a person, you will confront the person in a kind but firm way. Tough love must always be preceded by tender love, love is looking out for the other person's interest. [That] the step in trying to understand the behavior of [my husband], the inner motivations that drive him. The first step in becoming a positive change agent in [my] troubled marriage [was] to change [my] own attitude based on a better understanding of [my husband's] behavior. [This allowed me to] become free to take a new approach when [I] changed [my] thinking and [my] negative responses." I had a new appreciation for our marriage because I understood the root cause of our problems within our marriage. And because I understood that my husband and his behavior towards me and our marriage stemmed from his broken childhood, I had a new appreciation and love for him that no matter what we faced in our marriage and during our separations he strove to remain my husband and I his wife. I understood that the battle was not against him because the attack was on our marriage, the battle was against the devil. And I changed the method in which I handled and responded to my husband and our marriage. I pray more because I understand my position as his wife, as his rib. The line was drawn when God cursed Eve and the serpent. "I will put enmity between thee and the woman, and between thy seed and her seed; it shall bruise thy head, and thou shalt bruise her heel." Every time the enemy rose to bruise my heel, I had to get into my prayer position and bruise his head.

Part V

Reconciliation

Reconciliation – putting the rib back into place. Jesus as the doctor, taking His thumb and pushing me, my husband's rib back into place. Surround yourself with a positive circle of friends that are going to be honest with you and that are going to pray you and your spouse through, this is important because not everyone is for your marriage and you need to be careful of your conversations with others because you are in a vulnerable and fragile state concerning separation and you don't need anyone to speak against what God has spoken concerning your marriage. It is not always what is felt emotionally, but what did the Lord say, and how does the Lord want you to proceed concerning your marriage. Friends at times speak from an emotional place where they are, and project that onto your situation and that is not what God would have concerning your marriage. Be prayerful and allow the Lord to connect you with the individuals who again are going to pray you and your spouse through so that in God's time your marriage can be reconciled and healed.

How I received a forgiving heart

Early on I did a lot of things, I was very active in church, involved in ministry. I would pray prayers that I was not prepared for. I'd been asking God to give me a forgiving heart. I was pregnant with my youngest child and my husband admitted to me that he'd cheated. I'd had difficulty sleeping due to the pregnancy and being on bed rest, the look on his face, he appeared terrified. I'd first thought that someone died, but once he told me, I was like what, I was shocked and then angry. And he asked if I wanted him to leave. I started thinking unbelievable, here I was sitting there pregnant with your child, on bed rest and this was what you were out there doing, I was hurt, I felt like someone had taken my heart out and played soccer with it around my room. I did what I knew to do, I got on my knees and began to pray. I heard an audible voice, clear, and as if they were literally right next to me whisper into my ear, you asked me for a forgiving heart, now go forgive him. I stopped praying and began arguing with myself because God had already given a directive. God had already given me a word so that

A Dislocated Rib

was no longer about my husband cheating, but about an answered prayer and I didn't get to choose how God was going to do it. I had to forgive him completely.

I hadn't forgiven him at that time, which is why I told him to strap up when he went out. Reconciliation, making one consistent with another, to reestablish a relationship. I'd imagined that reconciliation meant that he would come home and we would be together and that would be the end of it. But reconciliation is a process. We'd learned new things about ourselves individually and we're learning how to come together and live in 'harmony', it is a process. Once I started to forgive him and accept him for who is, and not as a project, as someone I had to save, but as my husband. I prayed to God for God to give me a continued love for my husband. When I was totally convinced that my marriage would be reconciled. I had been bitter and I needed to feel that my husband was coming back to me. An actual marriage with the two of us as husband and wife engaging in healthy communication and living as husband and wife. Using [47]Gary Chapman's *Loving Solutions: Overcoming Barriers in Your Marriage* striving to not become the "dominating personality in [our] marriage, [understanding that we] cannot change [one another], but [that we could] influence [one another]. [Our] actions cannot be controlled by [our] emotions [or] the strongest emotion [which] is fear. [To] never use the power play approach, two people cannot play the game, [to] never use the submissive–servant approach, [to

---

[47] Gary Chapman
Loving Solutions: Overcoming Barriers in Your Marriage

not] yield to avoid conflict [because] it does not make for peace, [and to] understand that the highly controlling person is one who has taken the need for freedom too far [and] is only concerned for their own freedom and not the freedom of others, [to not become the] abusive controller, [but to] understand and respond to the [our] need for significance. [Understanding that] the self-worth of most controllers is tied to their performance. For the controller, failure to reach the goal is interpreted as "I am a failure "the inner needs for freedom and significance must be addressed by the spouse who would seek to be a change agent in influencing the controller. No arguments, instead, influencing by agreement[we] agree with [one another's] arguments but [we] don't allow [ourselves] to be controlled by those arguments. [And before you ask, no, this] does not strike at the self-worth or significance of [either of us], [but allows us to] play to [our] strengths [and] find the strength and maximize them because [we] are performance-oriented, [we] respond well to challenges to reach a given goal. [We] are task-oriented,[we] are willing to read books or attend seminars because [we] see this as a means of gaining information. [And to not become] the uncommunicative spouse [who] thinks that talking to other people about [our] problems is a sign of weakness [but] believes that they can solve their own problems."

I can remember when I began making preparation for my husband's return. The simplest things such as sleeping together in the same bed even though I've not slept on his side of the bed, cooking on a schedule rather than when I felt like it, cleaning and clearing spaces that I had come to occupy. And what it looked like as a whole when he returned. I wondered, do we have a conversation or do we just start? I came to a place where I learned that it was my needs and his needs, that [48]"much of our behavior in marriage was motivated by unmet emotional needs...

    Need for love (her)   need to be loved (him)
    Need for freedom   need to feel that he is number one

[These] are a learned behavior problem [and it is important to] find a way to meet [our] need for emotional love and at the same time maintain [our] own freedom. In a healthy marriage, [we] learn to meet each other's emotional needs, [we develop] a strategy for dealing with the conflicts [that will arise in our marriage.] The most common mistake [that we can make when we] are married to non-communicating mates is to focus on the silence rather than on the reason for the silence. [We had to understand that] old patterns are hard to break [and to take] assurance that [we were] there to listen, [and] not to condemn. [We learned] the art of sympathetic listening [where we] changed negative patterns of communication [because] negative communication patterns can silence [one another]." Reconciliation is not an easy process, but we learned that "complaining, cutting off, and not listening" were not effective in our marriage. We did as Chapman stated, we asked, "did[we] share how [we] would like things to be, did[we] allow/give space

---

[48] Gary Chapman
Loving Solutions: Overcoming Barriers in Your Marriage

How I received a forgiving heart

to [one another] or did[we] force communication, did[we] maintain confidences or did[we] broadcast [our] private conversations to others, did[we] openly share [our] own needs and desires in the form of requests rather than demands, did[we] give [one another] the freedom to have opinions that differ from [our] own or [were we] quick to set the [other] straight, [did we] give [one another our] focused attention, and did [we] communicate that the [others] words mattered to [the other]?"

But what truly helped me to reconcile with my husband and to prepare for the unknown of a reconciled marriage was the preached Word of God. I can remember on one occasion where I was asked to speak at a friend's church during a Woman's Conference. The topic that I preached that Sunday morning was Thriving Tainted Relationships. The premise was un-forgiveness and what it truly meant to forgive. Often times our relationships become tainted due to un-forgiveness and when things are not resolved, those relationships become thriving tainted relationships. I'd begun to share my story, my testimony of what God was doing in my life, in my husband's life, in our marriage during our last separation rather than ranting from an emotional place of all the things that I felt wrong during our last separation. The scripture that the Lord gave me to speak from, Matthew 5:23, set the tone for me in how to deal rightly with my husband and our marriage troubles. [49]Matthew 5:23,

---

[49] Matthew 5:23
The Message Bible

This is how I want you to conduct yourself in these matters. If you enter your place of worship and, about to make an offering, you suddenly remember a grudge a friend has against you, abandon your offering, leave immediately, go to this friend and make things right. Then and only then, come back and work things out with God.

In addition to prayer, I had to go to my husband in a spirit of love and gently but firmly confront our marital troubles. My problem was not my husband. My problem was the sin that was driving my husband's behavior. My husband was not my enemy, the devil was/is my enemy. And from this perspective confront in love my husband so that the Lord could reconcile us to the state of being married and not separated. And not so much immediately confront, I wanted to be spiritually prepared to confront my husband in the manner that the Lord would have me to confront him so that I did not give room to the enemy for further emotional distress and unresolved conflict. Allowing the Lord to lead me in the confronting process so that it was an effective process that would bring about a real change in our lives and not just another mask over it situation. In life, we cannot get what we need from God until we confront the matters that He would have us to confront. In prayer and preparation the Lord helped me to understand what true forgiveness was, and what it truly meant to forgive in my troubled marriage. To forgive was to restore a person back to the place that they were in your heart before they wronged you. I loved my husband, I married my husband, and he had been in my heart since we were in Junior High School. I had to forgive him back to the place that he held in my heart before we wronged each other. And just as Jesus casts our sins into the sea of forgetfulness, I had to cast my husband's sins and wrong doings into the sea of forgetfulness. Once I forgave him, once he was restored in my heart, I could no longer bring up the wrongs that we'd committed towards one another. I had to forgive him and ask him to forgive me so that we could move forward and begin to mend as God would have us to mend.

In our human state, it is a natural reaction to go fishing in the sea of forgetfulness so that we can hold wrongs committed against us to keep the other person in their place sort of speak. Or we tell people that we forgive them, but that we won't forget what they did to us when they hurt us so that that person cannot hurt us anymore. But that is not what the Lord would have us to do or be towards one another. You have to be spiritual even when your natural man wants to do something different from what God has spoken in His word. I couldn't fish for things to hold against my husband and I couldn't build up a wall to keep him from hurting me again. I prayed, I confronted, I forgave him, and the Lord restored us to the place that we should have always been: married. Another scripture that I shared with the congregation was [50]Hebrews 10:15-17,

Every priest goes to work at the altar each day, offers the same old sacrifices year in, year out, and never makes a dent in the sin problem. As a priest, Christ made a single sacrifice for sins, and that was it! Then he sat down right beside God and waited for his

---

[50] Hebrews 10:15-17
The Message Bible

enemies to cave in. It was a perfect sacrifice by a perfect person to perfect some very imperfect people. By that single offering, he did everything that needed to be done for everyone who takes part in the purifying process. The Holy Spirit confirms this: This new plan I'm making with Israel isn't going to be written on paper, isn't going to be chiseled in stone; this time "I'm writing out the plan in them, carving it on the lining of their hearts." He concludes, I'll forever wipe the slate clean of their sins. Once sins are taken care of for good, there's no longer any need to offer sacrifices for them.

In knowing the ultimate sacrifice that Jesus gave in order for us to be saved from sin, to no longer have a written plan on paper, but to have a relationship where the Lord dwells within us, in our hearts, where He wipes our slate clean once we accept Christ into our heart and those sins are no longer remembered. This is the place that I had to get to when forgiving my husband, forgiving myself as well, so that we can be the family unit that God always intended him and I to be. I had and have to operate always from the ministry of reconciliation restoring daily my husband back to the place in my heart before the wrongs. To say the least, where I preached to the congregation, I also preached to myself, my marriage, my situation. Deliverance came through the spoken word and I'd witnessed a platform being established for how I would go about the transition of my husband coming back to our home and my heart.

Another thing that prepared me for my husband's return and gave me some perspective for how it would be from both the wife and the husbands stance was a marriage blog/website that I'd come across,

How I received a forgiving heart

Rejoice Marriage Ministries. I found guidance and comfort in witnessing an actual couple who'd been in a similar situation as my own and reconciled in spite of the predictions that were projected against their marriage. One of the first messages that I'd read let me know that this was the experience that I could read about and learn from. There was vulnerability and honesty and rants and realness. Bob who was referred to as the prodigal husband wrote after reflecting on his reconciled marriage that, [51]"I think about some of the things I did, while pretending to be a Christian and cannot believe that it was me... it seems like only yesterday that I suddenly walked back into the home where we still live today, but as a remarried man." I imagined my husband having the same epiphany and I pondered the word remarried and what that experience would look like for my husband and I. The message further read, "I cannot look at the 20th anniversary of our remarriage without wondering how much different my life and Charlyne's life would be today, if she had followed everyone's advice and had given up on me. Yes, I could have convinced another woman that she needed me for a husband, but before long she would have also become a victim of my sin." This answered for me the male's perspective for how they see themselves in 'other' relationships. And I understood the more how important it was to have a positive circle of friends that would speak honestly into my spirit and life and not just tell me what I wanted to hear. I didn't take the unspoken or spoken advice of my peers in just moving on from

---

[51] Rejoice Marriage Ministries. God is Restoring Hearts, Lives, and Marriages. After the Prodigals Return. https://www.rejoiceministries.org/charlyne-cares-daily-devotional/2015/07/10/charlyne-cares-after-the-prodigals-return/

my husband. I stopped trying to get my husband to sign the divorce papers and I started preparing for the day that my husband would return to my heart and to our home. It was our marriage, it was our lives, and I was not going to give up on us so easily. Bob also wrote in his message, "the friends, pastors, doctors, and counselors were correct. Charlyne deserved someone better. God did not want her to continue living as she had been. But God, in His infinite wisdom, and according to His Word, did not give my wife a different husband. He gave her a new husband, in the same overweight, balding body of the man she had married in 1966... why did God do that? In answer to the prayers of a faithful, but forsaken, wife, who had taken a stand with Him, and chosen to swim against the tide of popular opinion... against the circumstances. My wife wanted to see our marriage problems fixed God's way." This was the space that I was in, I wanted my marriage fixed God's way. It wasn't my friend's decision, or anyone else's who had an opinion about our marriage in whether I stayed or left. It was God who brought us together and not even my husband and I could break that apart. I realized that I had still been standing for my marriage. And in still standing for my marriage, I came to understand that I needed to be consistent. One of the things that Bob spoke mostly about in his message was that his wife was consistent. He wrote, [52]"no matter what I said, no matter what I did, Charlyne stood firm that God was going to restore our marriage and rebuild our family. No matter what I needed, my wife

---

[52] Rejoice Marriage Ministries. God is Restoring Hearts, Lives, and Marriages. After the Prodigals Return. https://www.rejoiceministries.org/charlyne-cares-daily-devotional/2015/07/10/charlyne-cares-after-the-prodigals-return/

was willing to give all that she had… not once did I hear my wife threaten to give up her praying and standing for me." I understand even more so the vow that I'd taken, the covenant that I committed to and my purpose as a wife in standing with my husband. God had created me to be his help-meet and not his judge, jury, and prison. In understanding this I realized that my approach was not to be one of manipulation, but of one that was guided by God. And again, have the right circle of friends that will hold you accountable to your martial obligations. The notion of suffering is seen from a vantage point, every marriage will have moments of struggle, and just as with Job in the Bible, and can you not take suffering with happiness? Does the Lord not also ask us to suffer for His name sake? For it is in the suffering that the Lord will get the Glory and you will have developed and matured into a more matured fully functioning Christian and spouse. Divorce is not the end all, it needs to be the last resort.

I pondered what the return home would look like and I realized that as long as I always projected Christ then I my husband would return home as the prodigal son did, with a changed mind and a changed heart. And I would receive him as the father received his prodigal son, cover him, love on him in whatever state he returned, and be with him as he matured into the man of God that I know he has been called to be. I'd prayed for this day, and the Lord answered my prayer, the manifestation of that prayer was now in transit and I stood on the horizon sort of speak awaiting the day that I could put my arms around my husband and begin anew. [53]Gary Chapman in *Loving Solutions: Overcoming Barriers in Your Marriage* states that, "love is the most powerful weapon for good in [your marriage when you are at the] end of [your] emotional rope [and you have] drained energies. It is by means of positive steps that a marriage is changed. Most human behavior is motivated by the hidden self [where] motives are hidden [and] behavior that is motivated by internal physical needs is the easiest to observe and understand. Behavior motivated by psychological or spiritual needs is much harder to recognize. [That] exposing the hidden self is crucial for helping your spouse and your marriage. Understanding the motivation behind human behavior (illogical, hurtful, unreasonable, destructive)gives you helpful insight as you seek a new approach, insight into your own inner self as you evaluate your own behavior more realistically. Most human behavior is motivated by psychological or spiritual need. Physical and psychological needs are often intertwined, there's a deeper motivation driving the behavior. The closer you can come to understanding the internal motivation for your spouse's behavior the better equipped you are to be agents of positive change. How to meet those needs in a healthier manner in order to see a change in a positive direction, what is being said and what the other person hears [will be] different, [but] understanding the others motivation through communication the primary inner drives, needs, and desires that often motivate behavior."

---

[53] Gary Chapman
Loving Solutions: Overcoming Barriers in Your Marriage

Having a balance in our marriage where we complement one another and healthily support one another so that the other is receiving what they need to be effective in our marriage is key. I more wiser now in my conversations towards my husband because I understand that his brokenness and my position as his wife to not further break him, but to always project Christ to him and pray with and for him so that he overcomes his brokenness as I overcame my depression. It is the Lord that changes the manner in which we view things in our marriage. Having clear communication, gently confronting, being patient with one another, and always forgiving helps to keep so that we don't miss-communicate as often as we used to, I don't ask my husband to leave home, and we work through our differences. He is my husband. I am his wife. We are married. And I stand with him, we stand as one. Our family is a unit. And the devil has once again been defeated. What the devil thought would destroy my husband and I has made us more unbreakable. Bob in his message understood this for he wrote, [54]"our Lord changed me as I watched a wife who was consistently living for Him… Satan [didn't] leave town just because reconciliation [took place]… the homecoming that occurred in my life took place after one spouse learned to totally depend on our Lord in every situation. Because of this, there is now power and strength available to us as a reunited couple that can dispel any disruption that Satan tries to again throw in the path of our marriage… Satan is the enemy of marriage, we made a covenant with

---

[54] Rejoice Marriage Ministries. God is Restoring Hearts, Lives, and Marriages. After the Prodigals Return. https://www.rejoiceministries.org/charlyne-cares-daily-devotional/2015/07/10/charlyne-cares-after-the-prodigals-return/

one another that, regardless of circumstance, there will never be another separation or divorce in our home… should problems arise, [and] we will take them to God for His solution."

Hindsight is 20/20, but hindsight is also an opportunity to learn from the previous mistakes and turn. Hindsight gives you the opportunity to start anew with a fresh perspective because you've already seen the worse of what could happen. Hindsight is a gift that far too many do not take advantage of in marriages. I embraced my hindsight and I embraced my husband and we began our lives anew, whole, fully functioning, and married. I learned from Bob's testimony that Satan will continue to try and discourage my husband and I as we continue to reconcile, but that as long as we are honest with one another, the transitions will be positive and healthy. That in time, my husband will make the appropriate choices that will further bring us together where he will be able to disassociate completely from the 'other' women that he'd had relationships with. And that we need to focus on our children as well because they've seen my husband and I separated for so long that they may be defensive of me or him. We are a family unit. We include our children and our grandchildren so that they can see that God is God and that He is faithful to His people to do what He promises in their lives. The curse had been broken with my husband and I, our children and grandchildren were not going to succumb to the same fate that our parents or that we'd succumb to for a short period of time. Separation nor divorce were no longer options and topics of conversation in our home. My husband is my king and I love him the more because I went through a process where I learned and I experienced God in a real way, and now I apply all in my marriage. The things that drove us apart, that distanced us in our attempts are null and void. It is refreshing and interesting at the same time. The smile I smile is one of that says I've seen it and now I know what to do. It was never my job to rescue or change my husband. It was always my job to love my husband, be his wife and allow God to change us into the image that He would have us to be as husband and wife. Our home is our sanctuary, it is not a boxing ring and our bedroom is one of great intimacy and love because we have a new appreciation for one another.

I have a new perspective. And I realize even now that this is why I wrote this book, to break the cycle of broken marriages and the perception that certain behaviors is because a man is a man. No, God is God and in His time He makes all things new. Do not give up on your spouse. And believe God even when it is hard and always operate in a spirit of forgiveness.

Bibliography

1. Gary Chapman
   Loving Solutions: Overcoming Barriers in Marriage

2. Grace to You
   The Heart of Christian Fasting
   Part I: Fasting in the Old Testament
   http://www.gty.org/blog/B110107/the-heart-of-christian-fasting-part-1-fasting-in-the-old testament

3. Rejoice Marriage Ministries. God is Restoring Hearts, Lives, and Marriages. After The Prodigals Return.

4. https://www.rejoiceministries.org/charlyne-cares-daily-devotional/2015/07/10/charlyne-cares-after-the-prodigals-return/

5. King James Version

6. Message Bible

7. New International Version

8. HealDove. A Complete Guide to Dislocated Ribs: Symptoms, Treatment and Causeshttps://healdove.com/

injuries/A-Complete-Guide-to-Dislocated-Ribs-Symptoms-Treatment-and-Causes

9. Basic Protestant Vows

10. Wordpress.com

11. The Great Kamryn
http://www.goodreads.com/quotes/960187-the-truth-is-that-the-more-intimately-you-know-someone

12. Health line http://www.healthline.com/human-body-maps/ribs

About the Author

Minister D. Latrice is no stranger to overcoming adversity. She became a parent early in her teen years, married at the age of nineteen, and had three children by the age of twenty-five. In her debut as an author, she shares the wisdom she's gained to help others avoid and/or overcome the pitfalls that surface in even the healthiest marriages. She has been an associate minister at the Apostolic Faith Church for almost 20 years. D. Latrice received her degree in ministerial/Christian studies from Christian Life College in Mount Prospect Illinois. She prides herself on using the tools she learned from her studies as well as her church in the several counseling services she provides to family and friends. In addition to ministering and writing D. Latrice is a proud mother of three adult daughters and six beautiful grandchildren. D. Latrice resides in Chicago Illinois.

Footnotes

Gary Chapman
Loving Solutions: Overcoming Barriers in Your Marriage 1998

King James Version
Proverbs 18:21

King James Version
Proverbs 23:7

King James Version
Philippians 4:13

Revelation 12:11
King James Version

1 Corinthians 7:1-6, 10-17
New International Version

Matthew 19:1-11
New International Version

Basic Protestant Vows

Daniel 10:12-19
New International Version

Grace to You
The Heart of Christian Fasting
Part I: Fasting in the Old Testament
http://www.gty.org/blog/B110107/the-heart-of-christian-fasting-part-1-fasting-in-the-old-testament

1 Corinthians 7:5
New International Version

The Message Bible
Proverbs 5:20

King James Version
1 Thessalonians 5:22

King James Version
Romans 14:16

King James Version
Philippians 2:12

Health line
Ribs Pictures, Anatomy & Anatomy Body Maps – Health line
www.healthline.com> human-body-maps

A Complete Guide to Dislocated Ribs: Symptoms, Treatment and Causes
Hubpages.com

King James Version
Genesis 2:7-9, 15-23, 25

King James Version
Genesis 3:1-7

King James Version
Genesis 3:9-21

King James Version
Matthew 6:14-15

Matthew 19:5-6
King James Version

King James Version
Proverbs 4:23

New International Versions (NIV)
Mark 10:8

Footnotes

The Great Kamryn
Goodreads
http://www.goodreads.com/quotes/960187-the-truth-is-that-the-more-intimately-you-know-someone

King James Version
Matthew 19:6

King James Version
Matthew 5:44

King James Version
Romans 12:9

King James Version
Romans 3:23

King James Version
Ephesians 4:16

King James Version
1 Peter 4:8

The Message Bible
Matthew 5:23

The Message Bible
Hebrews 10:15-17

https://www.rejoiceministries.org/charlyne-cares-daily-devotional/2015/07/07/charlyne-cares